OHMS

On Her Majesty's Service

◆ FriesenPress

Suite 300 - 990 Fort St
Victoria, BC, Canada, V8V 3K2
www.friesenpress.com

Front cover crown icon created by Marie Ringeard from the Noun Project.

ISBN
978-1-4602-7593-1 (Hardcover)
978-1-4602-7594-8 (Paperback)
978-1-4602-7595-5 (eBook)

1. Biography & Autobiography

Distributed to the trade by The Ingram Book Company

Contents

Acknowledgements

I would like to thank my wife Rosemary for her help and advice, confirming dates, finding photos, sending them to my computer and encouraging me to keep working. Thanks to all the people I encountered during my fun-filled journey in the Army, schools, bands, churches, and of course my family, who have given me the ideas for my book. It would be impossible to name everyone, without leaving a few names out.

Finally, a word of praise to FriesenPress and Vanessa, my Account Manager, who guided me through the publishing process, answered all my questions and supported me through the project from start to completion.

To Charles Jeffery Parrott.

Introduction

Many of my friends have repeatedly urged me to write a book and share the interesting events in my life, in particular the time I spent in the British Army. Writing a book is a time consuming task, and if done properly can take a lot of research. The greatest hurdle that I had to overcome was finding the discipline to put my thoughts, stories, experiences, frustrations, struggles, failures, triumphs, and secrets down on paper, whilst being honest; deciding what to share and what not to.

It also occurred to me that perhaps the reading public would not believe some of my stories, and that my biggest dilemma was going to be, what do I leave out? There are events in my life that I would rather not remember, situations that perhaps I should not share. In spite of that, I would like to tell you about my life in great detail, and about the events that prompted me to join the British Army, and serve her Majesty.

Part I

CHAPTER 1

CHILDHOOD

I was born on 18 February, 1940, in Tolworth, Surbiton. After our father received his call-up papers and went off to join his regiment—the King Shropshire Light Infantry—my mother was left to raise my brother John and I. Later, we moved to Brighton, Sussex, in the hope that it would be safer away from the bombing; however, despite the war, growing up in Patcham was a happy experience.

Marjorie Anne and Charles William Scholfield – Mum and Dad

Mum and Dad visiting Osnabruck in 1963

Hitler started bombing England in September 1940, disrupting families and killing innocent civilians caught in the raids. The coastline was heavily defended with mines off the shore and barbed wire along the beaches. It would be two years after the war before the beaches would be safe for the public to use.

During the war, growing up in Brighton was quieter than living in London, except for the doodlebugs flying over on their way to the capital. They were intercepted by Canadian pilots flying spitfires patrolling the south coast, tipping the doodlebugs with the wings of the spitfire and sending them back out to sea. Listening to the drone, there was silence, followed by a loud explosion. I always wondered which building had been struck, and hearing sirens today brings back those wartime memories. I remember a cartoon I saw in Punch magazine, which depicted the thoughts of people during an air raid, with a large white house in a row of smaller houses. The caption under the cartoon was, "My house in an air raid".

Life was uncertain, living one day to the next and not knowing when the war would end. I did not know my father, who was away serving his country. My mother did a wonderful job looking after us, and coping with all the trials of war. In our street, everyone shared food, money, cigarettes, clothes, and furniture, and always had a positive outlook in every situation, with lifelong friendships formed between strangers. I have memories of my brother screaming from nightmares about German soldiers coming to take us away; he had packed a bag and came running into my room to protect me. During blackout times, we found our way round the house with candles and then made sure they were snuffed before going back to bed.

Our house on 113, Braeside Avenue was a semi-detached, flat-roofed house that had once been a school. There were doors—one on each floor—separating the two houses, which were eventually filled in to reduce the sound level between the two buildings. There were six of these buildings on our street in the town of Patcham. The back garden extended to a track, which surrounded cornfields over several acres up to 'Old Boat Corner', the junction of Ditchling Road and the corner of Stanmer Park. There were several stories about the name before the building of the A27 bypass. The first that there was reputedly a toll keeper's cottage or 'bothy' made out of an up-ended boat; another theory being that the name was a corruption of 'old boke corner'. While it had nothing to do with boats, it referred to the eighth century charter delineating the boundaries of the estate. 'Boke' is a Saxon word for book or charter. The third story, and the one I like best, was about a shepherd who farmed in the area and had died at the top of Stanmer Park. His dog had stayed at his side until he was found. The dog returned to the spot every day, so the local people placed an old rowing boat on its end as a shelter for the dog. When the dog passed away the boat remained for many years until it rotted away. You have a choice of three stories!

Along with several neighbours, my father fought against the building of the A27 bypass for twenty years; however, Council had its way and went ahead after the lobbying got weaker and eventually stopped.

My childhood was a happy one with lots of fond memories with friends and family. At Christmas our house was always full of relatives sharing the holiday, sleeping anywhere they could; my cousin Graham put cushions around the Westminster chime clock in the sitting room so that he could get some sleep. In those great years we had no TV or electronic devices to distract our conversation and party games. Our parents would gather in the sitting room with invited guests whilst we would be dressing up in my mother's bedroom, getting ready for a game of charades.

One Christmas morning as my brother and I opened the door we found a huge train set which our dad had spent many hours setting up; it ran between both rooms and was complete with all the signals, stations, level crossings, even complete villages with people. Later that afternoon, there were more presents under the Christmas tree, but this year there was another train set, which ran with a transformer. On Boxing Day we would visit our grandparents, who lived in the small town of Hassocks, which was a twenty-minute train ride from Brighton. We would visit at least twice a month, but eventually the failing health of my grandfather Henry forced them to move closer to us.

113 Braeside Avenue, Patcham, unchanged from 1940

The image above demonstrates that only one pillar remains at the entrance of our old home; the second pillar was demolished by our mother when, returning from the success of her driving test, she drove in at high speed. *Well done, Mum. At least you passed your test at the first attempt, whilst Dad failed his first try but succeeded on the second.*

When the siren went for an air raid we were rushed from our beds to the cupboard under the stairs for safety; warming our hands by a paraffin heater, we would get a biscuit and a hot drink before returning to our beds after the all clear.

I was awakened one evening from my bed, dressed, and taken over the fields at the back of our house to where a red cross plane had crash landed after being shot down. There were wounded soldiers being transferred to waiting ambulances.

There were German prisoners of war working, repairing the streets, who were chained together, manacled by the ankle and watched by mounted police guards carrying menacing batons. My mother wanted to ask them if they would like a cup of tea as she felt sorry for them but I don't remember her actually following through with this. Behind our house was a track later named the tank track after the Americans used the path for their vehicles. It was where I tasted my first American gum. The world was starving, food was scarce; there was no candy, jam, fruit or ice cream, and we all looked pretty thin! Growing up, my nickname was Gandhi; my ribs poked through my chest and my fingers and lips would turn blue when I went swimming. There was no need for Weight Watchers in those days. My favourite snack was a brown sugar sandwich and a breakfast treat was fried bread with dripping (cold fat).

I can remember birthday parties at Braeside Avenue with friends from school; sitting down together to listen to an instalment of Dick Barton (Special Agent), and his partner 'Snowy'. TV did not arrive in our house until 1953, but we were allowed to listen to selected radio programmes including Dick Barton and later the Goon Show. Entertainment in those years came in the form of family outings, walks and mushroom and blackberry picking (on the land just behind our house), going to the pictures (movies), enjoying a live play at the Theatre Royal, and of course, soccer and cricket. Transport was a bus or train for any long distance and everyone had a bike for local visits. On one visit to the Theatre Royal my mother and I were given the best seats in the house by the kiosk attendant who, after hearing our surname, thought that we were related to the famous actor Paul Scholfield. My mother just smiled and accepted the tickets.

Over the years our neighbours did not change that much; Mr. Phillip Billot, who was an amateur photographer, lived on one side, and the Coombs family lived on the other. Mr. Coombs had suffered as a prisoner of the Japanese and although he seemed fully recovered from the unspeakable physical torture he went through he still struggled with mental anguish. His business was very successful, a thriving pet food shop in Brighton. His two children, Peter and Rosemary, became close friends and were frequent visitors to our house. Some years later the Coombs family bought a bigger property and our new neighbour was a Mrs. Piesing, a single mother and her daughter Annabelle, who belonged to the Mormon faith. There was a constant stream of male visitors throughout the week "helping Mrs. Piesing find her way", so one of them had remarked to my mother. One morning at breakfast my father announced that he had heard moaning coming from next door the previous evening. Asking our father to explain, he said with a smile: "More men, more men!"

The upper bedroom next door was rented to a pleasant lady by the name of Miss Victoria Davies, who was a retired matron of Seaford College for boys. Her nephew, Michael, was visiting and came round to our house to play a game of chase, running through our house into our bedroom, on to the veranda and then jumping on to the coal bin in the back yard. My brother and I landed safely; however, Michael landed in the middle of the bin, which collapsed due to his weight. Fortunately, he was not hurt. My father remained calm when we told him about the collapsed coal bin and later he rebuilt it.

On another occasion we had invited some friends to the back garden to celebrate Guy Fawkes. All the families had pooled their fireworks and we were treated to a firework display. I found a rocket with a broken stick; setting it off at a low angle it streaked across the garden right between my father's legs (an incident to which he later referred as "the night he almost had his matrimonial prospects denied").

There were other stories which my mother would always tell about my childhood; the favourite being about when I was on a bus and had to pee urgently into a lemonade bottle she had provided for me. Then there was the time I had been helping my father paint the upstairs bedroom and I had told some guests that I had been using paint called 'Durex', when I had meant to say 'Dulux'.

Our neighbour Philip was invited round for beans on toast. My brother farted and Phillip responded by cupping his ear and saying: "Clear to come in on runway 2 now," to which we both howled with laughter. Our mother was in the kitchen, yet pretended not to hear. In fact, my brother was always farting and on one memorable occasion when we had adult company, he felt that he could not hold back and rushed out of the room. Unfortunately, as he opened the door to escape he let forth, grabbing everyone's attention. Whilst I could hardly contain my laughter, our guests expressed their shock and embarrassment.

Our house was always busy, especially during the holiday period, when we would have our friends and relatives come to stay. My mother was a great cook, and during the holidays we would often go to a pantomime, and then return home to an extravagant evening supper.

CHAPTER 2

PATCHAM PRIMARY SCHOOL

I went to school at Patcham Primary, which still stands and operates to this day some seventy years later. My memories of the school are happy ones. Miss Horsley was a kind but strict headmistress, who ran the school efficiently and was respected by pupils and teachers alike. I was not academically gifted, and was placed in the B stream of classes, which was the custom approach to education in those years. My talents were in the fine arts (music in particular), which were not considered core subjects and there was little support for them. I had little interest for mathematics or science but was fascinated with English Literature and history. The school timetable included dancing, which was fun. I was in a sword dance group, which we practiced every Friday, but I was paired off with Veronica Pocock a tall, red-headed girl whom I did not want to be near.

Veronica would wet herself at assembly, and although everyone felt sorry for her predicament, we would try to avoid close contact, for obvious reasons! The teachers were for the main part helpful, kind and fair with discipline. Pupils would never dare be disrespectful to a teacher in those days, not like the rudeness and poor attitude we see in some of our present pupil population. We were seen and not heard.

Each morning there would be an assembly, complete with hymn singing (*All things Bright and Beautiful*), *The Lord's Prayer*, and the reciting of the *Magnificat*, led by Miss Horsley in her tweed suit. There was another teacher, Miss Wennel, who would arrive at the school on a motorbike dressed with many jackets, scarves, galoshes, gloves and a huge helmet complete with goggles. It would take her at least twenty minutes to get dressed after school before braving the weather on her journey home some six miles from the school; she never missed a day of teaching!

There was one male teacher who always favoured the girls; at assembly one morning the headmistress announced that the same teacher had been promoted and was moving to a position in the north of England. The truth was that he had been dismissed for inappropriate behaviour with little girls! There was no proof but he should have been charged and sent to prison. One teacher who became my idol was Miss Muriel Hart, a young intern music teacher who encouraged me to play the violin, formed the first ever string group in a primary school, and formed the first amateur orchestra in Brighton, which eventually became the Brighton Philharmonic Orchestra; fifty years later, she was still involved as County Music Supervisor for Sussex.

I was sweet on a girl in my class; we were both six years old. I gave her a ring which I took from my home, not realising that it was my mother's engagement ring. Feeling embarrassed and anxious when my mother thought she had lost the ring, I confessed to my crime and made plans to get it back. Alas, the ring was lost. Miss Horsley paraded the whole school to search for the ring, which thankfully turned up in the grass of the playing field. This same girl who was always visiting in class missed the page number for homework; she asked me for the information and I turned round to give her the page number, receiving the strap for talking in class.

There was a short cut home that involved walking through the chalk pit; however, the teachers had warned the class about the dangers of taking this route and that we should avoid it. My friend and I took this short cut one afternoon only to have a group of older boys hurl rocks at us. We ran for shelter and hid in an old railway carriage, which had been dumped in the chalk pit, but we were pinned down for over an hour before we could safely continue. A lesson learnt from our venture was always to listen to the teacher. My brother found out the names of the bullies and gave them a good hiding.

I enjoyed soccer and was considered a useful bowler for the school cricket team. I came second at the county hurdle championships but had to bail out during a swimming event in the middle of the race after swallowing several mouthfuls of water.

Patcham School cricket team

My closest friend was David, who was a survivor of a serious school fire that had kindled in the wake of a plane crash, killing most of the school children and teachers. Jumping from a balcony with a teacher had saved David. However, he had suffered multiple burns and undergone many years of skin grafts, and only now was he able to cope with not being frightened of fire. It took many years for him to be able to attend a firework display on Guy Fawkes' night. David had a friend called Nina, an adopted child from Indonesia, whom I walked home from school with. The three of us would stop at the butcher's shop and pick up some sausage meat to eat on our way home, raw, uncooked and delicious. In those days a penny would buy an iced bun, a coloured drink, or a few slices of spam. School dinners were really not that bad and consisted usually of meat and potatoes followed by sago or tapioca pudding, or plums and custard. A drink could be bought for one penny at the grocer's shop, which was a bottle of water with a flavoured pill. At the bottom of the hill from Patcham Primary were a few shops, the Ladies Mile Hotel and a clock tower, which would sound the air raid warning for the town of Patcham.

At the bottom of the street from our house on Braeside was a small playing field where kids would gather for a game of football, but not on a Sunday when someone would confiscate the ball, get in a car and drive away. We were told later that this was the action of a member of the Lord's Day Observance Society trying to make a point; however, our football was returned with a note about playing soccer on the Sabbath! In the 1950s almost all the shops were closed on Sunday and it was a family day for most: rising late, enjoying a traditional Sunday lunch, a long walk or a joint picnic with another family.

In the spring I would cycle to Newtimber Woods and pick armfuls of bluebells and daffodils that were growing wild. I would rush home before they wilted, and then give them to my mother. With no TV, cellphones or electronic devices to entertain us, we found other inventive activities to occupy our time. We made camps with squares of turf piled up together, making a mini furnace from an old tin filled with coal and then cook up some potatoes to eat. Some days we would go to the stony beach of Brighton, brave the cold weather and spend three minutes in the sea followed by a thermos of hot tea as we shivered and huddled together. My first experience of a television broadcast was the Coronation of Queen Elizabeth in 1953 on a small black and white (snowy) screen with faint images appearing and disappearing, to which my father's comment was: "It's a sad day that we let that bloody box into our homes!" How right he was.

My father bought his first car in 1954—a Morris 11.9. HMK 64—which had been a company car for Expanded Metal Company of which he was Secretary. After my parents had passed their driving tests, it was my brother's turn to learn how to drive. However, he knew how to drive and scared all of us by slamming his foot down on the accelerator with my father yelling at him to slow down. I was too young and had to wait until I joined the Forces before I could take my driving test, yet there was a period when learner drivers could drive unaccompanied due to the Suez oil crisis in 1956. I took the car for a spin and, returning home, I was going too fast down Mill Hill Road and lost control of the car as it veered across the other side of the road, coming to a halt up a grass bank. Fortunately, there was no damage. I was badly shaken but was helped by a truck driver who had seen my performance and came to my aid. Having returned home, I parked the car. The look on my father's face was one of relief. I put on a brave face and denied any involvement, but I think I had learnt a lesson from this experience.

With my brother John

My final year at Patcham Primary ended with me failing the eleven plus exam for entrance to a Grammar School. I was now destined to return to the Secondary Modern part of the same school, which had a reputation for overcrowded classes, and daily fights, which was something I was not looking forward to. I spent just two weeks surviving at the senior school when my father suddenly appeared at my classroom and told me to pack my things.

CHAPTER 3

HOVE COLLEGE

My brother and I went for an interview at Hove College, a private school. I had to learn Latin with a tutor for a month, sit an entrance exam and was accepted. There was a totally different class of pupil at this college, mainly families with money. I think my grandfather assisted with the school fees as my father could not afford this. Hove College was a boys' only school with small classes, well-qualified teachers and situated by the sea front in Hove where I spent the rest of my schooling, graduating in 1956. *Thank you, Grandpa, for giving me a better education.*

Hove College—formerly Cliff House School—claimed foundation in 1796, which was demolished in 1934 when the school moved to Langton House, Hove College. This was essentially a boarding school, but 'day boys' were growing in numbers and later became the majority. The school was divided into four houses with names of previous headmasters. I was placed in Avery, the name of a headmaster in 1886.

In 1951, King George VI died peacefully in his sleep and the announcement was made at the school. We were in our Lower third classroom, and were told to stand as the teacher proclaimed: "The King is dead. God save the Queen." Classes were dismissed, which meant that our afternoon was free to go to a movie; however, everything had closed down as a mark of respect. Arriving home with no homework, I turned on the radio and found every channel playing sombre music, replacing the scheduled programmes.

Paul Montri and myself as a duo

My soccer days

The school had a system of awarding merits and demerits placing a board in public view on the main landing. For excellent work or gentlemanly conduct a star was awarded; however, for poor work, attitude or behaviour, a round was awarded. At the end of each month a tally was taken and the house with the most merits would be given a Saturday morning holiday. Our school week included sport on Wednesday afternoons and school on Saturday mornings. Towards the end of each month everyone was on their best behaviour and producing excellent work. Our school uniform was a maroon blazer with silver edging, and on the breast pocket was an image of a Chinese Junk with the words "Rege Recte" (Steer Straight) inscribed beneath.

There was an old, out of tune piano in the lower third classroom on which I would play hymns for assembly during the week. I remember one line from the school song: "Guile with meretricious glamour". I doubt that my present grandchildren would know what that meant. Ironically the headmaster, Cameron Jackson and J. Dickson were both agnostic. Pupils mainly came from wealthy families with most of my classmates from a Jewish background, with names like Siefert, Katz, Grossman, Shane and Shoebridge, who were good friends. My closest friend, however, was Paul Montri, son of the financial advisor to the King of Siam. Paul received an allowance each month from his father, which he generously shared with all of us taking a large group of our class to a café on the seafront to enjoy a cup of Horlicks.

As a senior student I was made a prefect, which entitled me to wear a black blazer in place of the maroon jacket with the silver braid and use the prefect's staff room where I could smoke. Smoking in the 1950s was socially acceptable with our headmaster actually smoking in the classroom while teaching European history.

There were many pranks and dares played at the college. I have a recollection of a pupil who had turned the main switch for the gas supply off and on, thus causing each gas fire in the ten classrooms to blow out with a good bang. Another prank was to try to run up the masters' stairs without being caught, and although I was successful every time, I got a few suspicious looks from some teachers. Of course mimicking teachers was the favourite. Despite being told repeatedly that he would never make it, Peter McEnery went on to become a successful actor. He started at the bottom of the ladder, sweeping the stage, etc., yet, his first real break came when Andrew Ray—son of Ted Ray—was sick. Peter took his part and later appeared in a film with Brigit Bardot, while his greatest achievement was being selected to play Hamlet.

Teachers at the college were knowledgeable and helpful; most had a Master's degree. Mr. Gubert, who was an Austrian, had a PhD. (LLD) Vienna. A Doctor of Law, who taught mathematics and French. My geography teacher was Francis Browne, a Monk from Cowfold Monastery, who was very strict and hardly ever managed a smile. That was until he fell in love with a nurse; he left the monastery, got married and was a changed man! Mr. Browne had a keen sense of smell and was continually complaining about the stale odour in our classroom. We hid a sour bottle of milk under the floorboards. He got so mad one day that he called the headmaster to come and smell the classroom for himself. But as soon as he left the room, a student removed the milk and sprayed the classroom, while hiding the bottle outside. Unfortunately for him, he was caught in the act and our game was over.

My teacher for English Literature was a Mr. Sellers, who was ex-Governor of Wandsworth Prison. He was able to make books come alive. We were reading *Richard II* by Shakespeare; *Androcles and the Lion* by Bernard Shaw, and *The History of Mr. Polly* by H.G. Wells. I only wished I could have found the same enthusiasm for my other subjects. *Thank you, Mr. Sellers, for showing me the enjoyment of English Literature.*

My middle school teacher was Mr. Ormowe, a white Russian, who became my violin teacher. He was very gifted, speaking four languages: English, French, Russian and Hebrew. In addition to holding a diploma L.R.A.M. for playing the violin, he had won many trophies as an international chess champion. He and his wife adopted six children from a local orphanage and was liked by all the students with his knowledge and sense of humour. Sadly, he fell victim to cancer and died at the age of forty-two; it was a devastating loss to all of us. My interest in playing the violin seemed to flounder after his death, despite finding two other teachers, both of whom died one after the other. Hopefully it was nothing to do with my playing that caused their death! My teacher entered me in the Brighton Music Festival in a violin class with fifteen other contestants all playing the set piece *In Pensive Mood* by Molly Paley. I had no accompanist, and was standing in the wings of the theatre shaking like a leaf. I marched on and played the opening note, Eb, fourth finger on the A string with an incredible vibrato. I finished the work and was placed second for my vibrato and courage.

My school reports were really quite disappointing, beginning in the lower third classroom from, "Michael has worked conscientiously and made very good progress, although his academic gifts are not great (which really meant that they thought I was thick!)," to the fifth form with, "Good progress has resulted from keen interest, despite inconsistent effort; if he relied upon his own judgement of values, he would progress more rapidly." However, remarks in sport were more encouraging: "Pillar of support, most valuable as an organiser, a promising footballer and a good cross-country runner." My worst marks were in Latin (22), French (41) and physics (21), while my best marks were English Literature (88), history (90) and spelling (97).

As far as I can recollect, my father was an agnostic and my mother a lapsed Anglican. Neither of them were churchgoers, yet I became involved in badminton at the local church hall and went to Anglican church services with my group of friends, listening to the wisdom of the Reverend Garston Smith, an Australian, who we referred to as "Ghastly Smith". I was confirmed on the 25 November, 1956, by the Bishop of Lewes, but fell away from the church with the exception of some visits to a baptist church, when I was courting the daughter of the minister. I finally graduated from Hove College, excelling in the fine arts, music, English Literature and European History. My graduation ceremony consisted of being congratulated by the headmaster, Cameron Jackson, followed by the burning of my school blazer on the beach at Hove.

CHAPTER 4

LIFE AFTER THE WAR

The war continued throughout 1944, yet there were signs of an end in sight. My brother and I went to visit our father, who was in a hospital in Shrewsbury with sciatic nerve problems. Meeting him for the first time in my memory, he was dressed in hospital blues with a red tie, which meant that he was an up patient and due for release. Standing by his bed, holding something behind his back, he handed me a model racing car and my first orange. He was surrounded by less fortunate servicemen; having been rescued from a sinking torpedoed ship, some of them were dying from oil in their lungs. At least my father was coming home—where many did not return.

Germany finally surrendered, and the war came to an end. My wife's father was a POW for four years, of which, he rarely spoke of until many years later. He was reported missing, and later presumed dead. He was eventually found alive in a camp, yet at half his normal weight, so he had to spend a year on a special farm in the west learning how to eat normally before he was able to return to standard living.

There was a street party held to celebrate peace, with tables made from the air raid shelters from our homes, hundreds of people sat to enjoy what food they had. I have never seen anything quite like this, since. After our meal we climbed on open top buses, where we waved flags and cheered as we were driven around the streets of Brighton.

My father was demobbed, and arrived home to further celebrations. He now had the task of bringing his family together and getting used to normal living. I distinctly remember walking with him on a Saturday morning, down Bengairn Avenue to buy a box of Quality Street, and a sixpenny bunch of violets for my mother. What a perfect gentleman.

I have many childhood memories of long walks to Ditchling, followed by afternoon tea at Anne Boleyn's cottage; pantomimes with supper before at the Tatler Tea Rooms (Baked beans on toast), and on special occasions we would be treated to a three course meal at Langford's restaurant on the Western Road, Brighton. My choice of meal would be the mixed grill!

My father was Company Secretary of the Expanded Metal Company, and succeeded his father, both working for thirty-five years as the senior accountant. He travelled daily from Brighton to London, working in the city of Westminster. He had studied at the LSE (London School of Economics) and had been influenced by the political thoughts at this school, developing leftist beliefs. Many of his professional friends had similar thoughts, but had to hold secret meetings to discuss their views. They read the *Daily Worker*, classed as communist literature in the 1950s. I can remember my father standing by the 'Peace Statue' in Hove, giving public speeches about peace. He was being harassed and yelled at by ignorant crowds, yet he stood his ground, determined to spread the message. He had also joined a group of leftist thinkers, who formed the BSFS (British Soviet Friendship Society,), which sponsored Soviet dance and singing groups to the UK. Private meetings were held in Brighton at the People's Book Shop.

I went to several of these gatherings with Soviet dancers and singers performing. The famous Paul Robson agreed to come as a guest singer, but because of his communist leanings he was denied a decent concert hall for his performance, so a local church offered their hall for the night.

All of the friends of my father were intelligent, sincere and professional people, who were not going to be duped by the current Tory British Government; all of them voted Labour. My father played the violin and piano and spent many hours working with me as a beginner on the violin. He had perfect pitch, which he passed on to me, and later I passed this gift to Alex my youngest son. I bought a recording of the first *Symphony in C Major* by Beethoven as a birthday gift for my father, however, as soon as it started to play we both looked at each other and knew this was not C Major; it was Db, a semitone out. I returned the record to the shop and received a refund. We would announce keys as we listened to music from the radio.

My mother had a happy childhood, marred by the early death of both her mother and father, which resulted in her going to live with her eldest brother George. Uncle George and his wife Wynn lived in Kingston, where he worked as a manager of the Kingston Dairy. The Dairy consisted of horse drawn carts, which delivered the milk to local residents. Aunt Wynn would visit our house in Brighton, always making a trip to the seafront and of course Brighton Palace Pier.

Posing on the Palace Pier with Aunt Wynn

I woke one morning remembering a vivid dream I had about a large house, and recalled the details with my mother over breakfast. There was a large garden with chestnut trees and a badminton net set up. There was a river at the bottom of the garden and a boathouse. I described each room in the house and the bathrooms.

About a year later our family was invited to stay with my father's cousin in Staffordshire and as we arrived at the house, both my mother and I knew that this was the house in my dream. "How could that be? Probably just coincidence!" my uncle exclaimed. That night I made my way to the bathroom but instead, found myself in a room full of boxes of apples. I tried another door and eventually found the toilet. At breakfast I relayed my story to everyone; my uncle went pale and then informed me that the room with the apples had originally been a washroom when he had first bought the house!

CHAPTER 5

AUSTIN REED

I always wanted to be involved with music and had considered enrolling at one of the music schools in London, but after sending applications to several schools it became very clear that neither I nor my parents could afford this sort of venture.

Looking at the job market in Brighton I went for an interview as a junior salesman with Austin Reed Ltd, a high-class men's tailors from Bond Street London. To my surprise I was selected for the position, turning up for my first day in a smart suit and not quite knowing what to expect. It was not long before my military musical career would begin, although there were some amusing events, which took place before I joined the British Army.

The manager of the Brighton branch of Austin Reed was an Irishman called Mr. O'Keefe, who was a gentleman and liked by all the staff. My position as junior was to vacuum the carpet, tidy tie and sock trays and would be granted permission to sell the same to a customer. Within a week I was selling shirts and earning some commission to boost my meagre salary of £3.00 a week. I gave my mother ten shillings for room and board, spending the remainder on myself, which included taking out a young lady to the pictures followed by a hamburger and coffee in a Wimpy bar.

There were three members of staff apart from me. Mr. Champion (assistant manager), Mr. Crabtree (bespoke tailor), and Mr. Marriott our shirt salesman. Joan was our office girl, and Joe the porter, sent out our parcels. At tea break, we would go to the basement and visit sharing our morning. Mr. Tony Crabtree was shocked to hear that my weekly salary was only £3.00 a week, and encouraged me to ask for a raise. Response to my request was immediate, after a senior executive took me out to lunch from London; my pay was doubled to £6.00 a week! Mr. Marriot was chosen to work on the Queen Mary working in the Austin Reed shop. The trip from Southampton to New York enabled him to see a live stage production of *My Fair Lady* and on his return we were treated to all the songs from the show sung by Mr. Marriot, until we had to ask him to shut up! I became good friends with Tony Crabtree and it was through our conversations that he later encouraged me to think about joining the British Army.

A month passed and a new staff member was hired. Norman Lefton came from a wealthy family and on his second day he invited me to go for tea by car to Rottingdean some two miles away. "How on earth are we going to do that in twenty minutes?" I asked. He then showed me his latest car, a TR6, which he assured me would have no problem getting there and back with time to spare (travelling at 100mph, just for tea!).

It was at this time I met Annette, a young girl who worked for a Jaeger shop on the same street. We became friends, and began dating. We were both invited to a party given by her boss who was arranging for both of us to stay the night. After phoning my mother—who was not keen on the idea—our plans changed. I missed the last bus home and had to walk.

On the following Monday there was a visit by a window dresser who got me to stand like a statue in the front window, wait for people to stand looking, then scare them away. He took me out for afternoon tea, where he sat feeding imaginary dogs from the table as customers looked on shaking their heads. Before he left for London, he insisted that I place a bet on three horses which he knew would win.

I had never bet on horses before and was slightly reluctant, but he assured me that if I did not win, he would give me my stake back. He gave me the names, Two Blues at Kempton Park 2:00pm race, and Sea Blue at the 3:00pm at Lewis and one other at 3:30pm. The bet was a special deal, which would place the winnings from the first horse on to the second and again to the third. All horses just needed to be placed first. I could only afford five shillings and had to place my bet illegally with a bookies runner who sold newspapers outside the Odeon Cinema by Austin Reed shop. Later that evening, checking the results, I discovered that I had won a considerable sum of money, which was equal to six weeks of my salary! I was jubilant and phoned to thank him. His reply was: "Told you to place more money on your bet." I often wonder how much he placed that day. I went to pick up my winnings and gave the runner a handsome tip.

Oddly enough, I have never won money on horse racing since, and put my windfall down to beginner's luck!

CHAPTER 6

JOINING THE BRITISH ARMY

My time with Austin Reed was coming to an end. I received my first pay raise and returning from lunch I passed an Army Recruiting Office, which had a sign saying: "Join the Army and get your career paid for". I made some enquiries and found out that I could get a musical education paid for in return for a few years of service, which sounded like a good idea to me.

At the recruiting office it was arranged for me to have an interview with the Band of the Household Cavalry in Windsor. My interview was a total disaster. I was separated en route after getting on the wrong half of the train, with my half going to another destination. I arrived for the interview thirty minutes late, and I was asked to sight read a difficult piece for violin, which did not go well. I did not like the attitude of my interviewer who asked me to return at another time.

Arriving back in Brighton I explained my dilemma to the recruiting officer who persuaded me to join the Royal Fusiliers City of London Regiment, best known as the 'London Irish Black Watch' called because there were a lot of coloured and Irish gentlemen in the regiment. Later as a member of the band recruiting in London, our bandmaster was asked by the colonel how many recruits had signed up that day. The reply was, "Six, sir. Three black, one white and two Khaki."

Our colonel replied: "Have to look into that, bandmaster, we are only allowed two percent in the regiment!" I discovered later that the reason for this Queen's Regulation Rule was because they clan! In present times this would be considered racist but not so back then.

All that remained for me to do now was pass a medical exam and sign on the dotted line for three years as a regular soldier. The medical exam consisted of undressing and standing naked whilst a female nurse grabbed my testicles and asked me to cough. This was followed by a hearing test, which had me stand in the corner of a darkened room (fully clothed) waiting for a doctor to whisper something from behind me. Sitting with other new recruits drinking tea in the hope we would be able to give a urine sample one of the recruits drank the tea and them promptly went to the washroom without giving the sample. Everyone had a good chuckle over this, just how thick was he, I thought. I passed all the tests with no problems and proceeded to sign on for three years.

I now had the task of breaking the news to my parents, who would not be keen on my serving in the British Army. Having already experienced the horrors of war, I knew how my father would react. However, after explaining my reasons for my actions he was quite positive and wished me well, but I think my parents were disappointed that I had failed to discuss the matter with them prior to signing up.

The following week I resigned from Austin Reed to which the manager replied: "Mr. Scholfield, you're a bloody fool," and then gave me lecture about the wonderful career prospects I would be missing at Austin Reed. Some ten years later I was conducting my first band in Cheltenham and having some free time went shopping and found a branch of Austin Reed Ltd. I discovered that the manager was Mr. O'Keefe when I saw him standing on the shop floor. He failed to recognise me until I approached him and said: "No milk, two sugars, that's how you like your tea isn't it?"

Leaving Austin Reed I was to report to the Tower of London (home of the fusiliers), the following week on 10 December, 1958.

CHAPTER 7

TOWER OF LONDON

I was to go to the Tower of London for a one-day orientation, return for Christmas and then re-join the regiment in January. I boarded a train at Brighton Station heading to Victoria, and looking out the carriage window as the countryside went by I thought, *What have I done?* It was too late to turn back *or was it?* I guess I was apprehensive due to the fact that all my friends had such a negative view of the Army and at a farewell party one of my friends said, "What do you expect to gain from this? It will not be what you think." My father was not keen on my joining although he had not said anything; I knew from his experience in the King's Shropshire Light Infantry in the last war.

The food was inedible, sleeping arrangements were bunk beds. If you were on the lower bunk, you risked being sprayed with urine from the top bunk and the average intellect was low, as few soldiers had any formal education. He told me that the RSM of his regiment was illiterate, signing papers with an X, and his command of the English language was limited; mostly vulgar expressions were the only words in his vocabulary. "F...ing Hell" was his most favourite term, and as a result his subordinates knew him as Sgt. Major K'nell. Surely things had improved by now!

Tower of London – Royal Fusiliers Depot 1958

The train arrived at Victoria and I walked to the underground boarding a tube to Tower Hill. The Tower is visible from the station. I approached the main gates, showed my pass and entered the Tower walking past the White Tower and Traitors Gate to the Orderly Room. Here I met a group of National Servicemen who had reported to serve the mandatory two years. There were forty of us in the new intake who were given an extensive tour of our new home, followed by lectures from our drill sergeant. This was followed by lunch, which was really good and our afternoon consisted of introductions to the RSM, the adjutant, second in command and finally our commanding officer. Each one of us was given an interview and finally sent home on leave without pay and a warrant to return on 5 January, 1959, spending my last Christmas at home before joining the Army.

CHAPTER 8

BASIC TRAINING

My stay at the Tower and later, Purfleet (the training camp) was memorable, amusing- unforgettable-unbelievable, and something I'm glad I experienced.

Our first parade in civvies, opposite the building with the crown jewels, was listening to our training sergeant and his two corporals who were going to be with us for the next eight weeks. Staff Sergeant Siminot had a large wart on his right cheek, which was difficult not to look at when talking to him, and his two corporals were like sheep dogs running around barking orders at us. We were marched everywhere, even to meals, which seemed quite pointless at the time. Our first task was getting 'kitted out' at the clothing store where we stood in line and were handed pile after pile of clothes, bed linen, blankets, mug, knife, fork, spoon, mess can, two pairs of boots and a kit bag. Our uniforms were the old 'hairy' battle dress, denim order for fatigues, a beret and a steel helmet. We had PT Kit, draws, cellular, braces, socks, tie, patent 57 belt, shirts, gaiters, and a housewife (mending kit). We were expected to repair holes in our socks!

Sizing was not a priority of the clothing store man, who looked you up and down, took a guess at your size and then hoped that everything would fit. My beret was really big but I was shown how to shrink and shape it by soaking it in boiling water the following day. There were eight beds to each room and I landed up with five men from Liverpool (all national servicemen), one regular soldier and a cockney, who knew everything about everything! The floors had to be polished with a bumper, the washrooms spotless, our beds with hospital corners, place our kit in our lockers at ninety-degree angles, dress in denim order and stand to attention by our beds. When approached by Staff Sergeant Siminot, we were expected to recall our regimental number: 23686017, something I have never forgotten! "Change into battle dress order, come on, move yourselves!" came the order from the corporal. We changed, raced down the stairs, formed up with the other squads in close order formation, and the fun was about to begin. We spent the next hour marching up and down the square as directions for halting, stepping off and saluting were barked at us as we crashed into one another trying not to laugh. Two offenders were picked out and our friendly staff sergeant came up to them, his face one inch from theirs saying: "It's no good looking up at your maker, 'e can't help you now!"

Someone whispered: "Don't look at his wart," and the squad fell about laughing. Drill parades were three times each day and with practice we slowly improved over the next few weeks.

The NAAFI (Navy, Army, and Air Force Institutes) was our only retreat where we could drink vast amounts of tea and gobble the delicious pastries on offer. Fifteen-minute break followed by another session of drill and mercifully lunchtime came followed by some rest. The food was edible but tasteless and I would take lots of potatoes and gravy at lunch, not trusting the greens after the cook found a dirty dishrag at the bottom of the pan. And of course there was the Army favourite, corned beef. The best meal of the day—if you were up early enough—was breakfast, with a choice of porridge or cereals, followed by bacon and eggs cooked in front of you, and plenty of it.

The afternoon session were lectures about rules followed by more rules, in particular, saluting officers. *Never walk across the parade ground.* We were told that this was sacred ground. As soon as the lecture had finished we were rushed to our quarters and the order was: "Change into PT Kit, you are going on a short run," which turned out to be four miles down to the moat surrounding the Tower and back to the parade ground four times, finally returning to our barrack rooms to rest and get ready for supper.

The food again was plentiful but with little taste. We were not permitted to wear civilian clothes yet, but we were told that this privilege would be granted when we went home on our first long weekend pass.

Our evening entertainment was, sitting on our beds bulling our best boots followed by lining up to use the one iron between two rooms (sixteen recruits). The other regular soldier in our room showed us how to wet the crease in our BD trousers by sliding the crease between our lips, placing it under the mattress and then sleeping on it. This was an excellent alternative and not only looked good but got us to the NAAFI first. This is where the drinking began, tongues loosened and stories were swapped. The bar closed at 21:30, staff parade was at 22:00 and lights out (last post on the Bugle) at 22:30.

I remember my first night seeing grown-up men crying with their head in their hands missing the comforts of home but all of us were exhausted and soon drifted into a deep sleep.

Communal living brings out the best and worst in everyone with personal hygiene being top of the list apart from stealing. One of our squad did not shower too often and as a result smelt of body odour. Six recruits stripped of his clothes and treated to a "Regimental scrubbing" with a large bass broom. He showered twice daily after this occurrence.

We awoke the following morning to the sound of Reveille followed by our training corporals shouting, "Good morning, gentlemen. Hands off cocks and hands on socks, come on move it!" If you got out of bed immediately you stood a good chance of making the showers without a line up and also put you in the front of the breakfast queue. Within the first week I would shower and shave at night using an electric shaver in the morning, which put me in front most of the time; however, I could get washed, shaved and dressed in seven minutes. Studded boots could be heard clattering on the metal stair treads as we ran downstairs on our way to breakfast of bacon and eggs, toast and a mug of very sweet tea. Then, back upstairs ready for room inspections, first by our friendly corporal followed by the beloved Staff Sergeant Siminot. After several adjustments to our lockers we were chased down the stairs: "On Parade!"

The first order of the day was the inspection of the squads after we had spent many hours bulling boots and pressing uniforms in the hope of passing the test. Most of us were in the clear but there were always a few who did not match up. One soldier had used shellac for the toecaps of his boots, which looked great but when he slammed his foot to attention the toecap flew off his left foot. It must have been hilarious to watch us. I was ordered to have yet another haircut, finally having a crew cut to satisfy their demands, which actually looked very smart and I have liked the idea ever since.

We all had personal interviews with our commanding officer who was helpful in placing us within the regiment. I had already decided to become a bandsman; my schooling had been good and I had passed some G.C.E. exams on graduation. Apparently, I was the only soldier in the intake with any significant schooling. It was suggested that I become an officer but I declined explaining that music was my passion and that was the reason for joining to gain experience in a band.

It was the month of January, cold, wet and windy. We ran five miles followed by a *cold* communal shower with lots of horseplay. Already there was a bond between us with people assisting others when they needed help. We were marched to the armoury issued rifles (the Belgian Rifle) and began rifle drill. After the first morning session we went to the NAAFI for a break; leaving my rifle against the wall I went to the toilet and when I came out my rifle had gone. Trying to explain the situation to the corporal he screamed at me and had me placed in open arrest and marched to the Guard Room. Apparently I had committed a grave sin. *Never leave your rifle where you cannot see it!* It transpired that the training sergeant had seen it and confiscated the rifle. I was marched in front of the colonel who listened to the charge but ruled in my favour as case admonished; however, events really were in my favour because I was going to be a bandsman and strictly non-combatant I was to be excused rifle drill. I had a free period when rifle drill was posted and did not attend any lectures on weapon training.

Looking back on those days it seems as though we all had a lot of fun and life was sharing the moment without our cell phones or Facebook. We were able to be present to one another without technology; just really living the moment and having a lot of fun. There was comradeship between all of us, looking out for each other. Some of the daily routine was full of silly things, which caused side-splitting agony. There was not a day that went by without something to laugh about. I was ordered to clean a window, which was thirty feet at the top of a building. I found a ladder and began to climb when one of my friends stopped me, took the ladder and smashed the window. "Looks pretty clean to me now; we can't have you falling off the ladder, can we?"

We were approaching the fourth week when we would be given a forty-eight-hour pass to go home. In discussion with other recruits we had all noticed our libido was low or non-existent. None of us had any sexual desires and were sleeping eight to nine hours each night. However, we found the culprit and it was the *tea!* It had bromide (Saltpeter) in it! We all changed to cold drinks after this discovery. My leave was approved; I left the Tower in uniform and made my way to Brighton, and felt proud to be wearing the uniform of the Royal Fusiliers with the white hackle sprouting from the cap badge. Going home meant mother's food, and how I had missed it. I spent my weekend visiting with my old civilian friends who were, I think, surprised that I was enjoying my stay at the Tower, and my first taste of OHMS. My parents were also glad to see that I had made the right decision, well at least, so far!

CHAPTER 9

PURFLEET CAMP

On my return to the Tower, I just missed a tube train at Victoria, caught the next, and then finally arrived after midnight. However, the gates were shut at midnight, so I went back to Canon Road Police Station where I was given a cell for the night, a cup of steaming tea (without the bromide), and an early call at 6:00 when the gates opened. I had a shower, breakfast, cleaned up and made it for the first parade. Punishment for minor misdemeanours, particularly being late for a parade, was a restriction of privileges. I was late for a sick parade because I felt so ill and had a high fever, yet was still charged. I was awarded three days R/P. I had to clean kitchen floors, wash dishes, clean toilets and finally I was made to scrape a six-foot table with a razor blade. This cut my hands but my fever had gone.

The final insult was the staff parade at 22:00. I was inspected and then returned to my barrack room to clean my kit, ready for the morning inspection. I was never late again for any parade for the next seventeen years!

We were leaving for Purfleet Camp the following week. Purfleet had the reputation of being a cold unpleasant camp, which our training sergeant had described as "rustic". Our time would be spent with cross-country runs of seven miles (daily), night exercises and weapon training on the range. Our accommodation consisted of Nissen hut, a tunnel-shaped hut of corrugated iron with a cement floor, heated with a coke stove and furnished with luxurious camp beds. It was February and the weather was damp and cold. It was at this "rustic" camp that we learnt how to make sure the fuel for heating did not run out. The secret was to poach some from another hut and then paint our supply with whitewash to prevent stealing. I went to sleep that first night dressed in my great coat because of the cold. I could see my own breath!

The food at Purfleet was lots of beans, cabbage and sprouts, which set the stage for multi-farting later that evening. We had a contest to see who could actually fart a tune. One of our comrades, who was over 6 feet and weighed 220 pounds called Rupert, could actually rip out British Grenadiers, but only the first four bars. I could not stop laughing and even today when I hear this tune I am reminded of that hilarious evening. We called our phantom farter "Rupert the Bear". Despite the cold and rundown camp, we ached from laughing almost every day. Living and working together brought out the best and worst in all of us; there was a spirit of working together, helping each other and sharing our gifts.

On our third day we were to go on a night exercise, but most of us had colds and in particular hacking coughs. Our fearless leader Staff Sergeant Siminot gathered us for a briefing, which went something like this: "All right you 'orrible lot; tonight is your night exercise and silence must be kept, otherwise the enemy are going to know where you are. Right now, all 'ave a good cough before we get started!" It was on this exercise that one of the soldiers could not stop coughing and was complaining about the intense cold. Staff Sergeant Siminot hit him on his helmet with a rifle butt and said: "Think warm." Everyone fell about laughing. The Army mentality was really hilarious, yet practical, especially in times of war although there were many jokes about this way of thinking. The best I heard was about the mentality of the Guard Regiments. Guardsman Jones's mother dies and the adjutant orders the RSM to convey the news: "Guardsman Jones, your mother's dead!" Poor Jones, he is in shock; a week later his father dies of a heart attack, and the adjutant warns the RSM to be diplomatic this time, when speaking to Jones: "B Company, on parade. All those with fathers, one pace forward; not you, Jones, he's dead."

The last Friday at our "rustic" camp, we were permitted to go into town for a few drinks. This was not a good idea as some of the locals picked a fight with one of the recruits who was talking to a girl, which resulted in a full-scale punch up. Our fine lads from Liverpool thrashed the local lads but did not cause any damage to the pub.

The following week was to be our last at Purfleet, beginning on Monday firing the Bren gun and the Belgian rifle on the range. I was included in this activity despite my previous encounter with a rifle. I went on the range and lay down by a Bren gun. I had not had any weapon training like my fellow comrades so I just tried to copy what the soldier was doing beside me. This seemed easy enough; there was really nothing to it. What I did not realize was that there were two positions on the gun, single and rapid. Mine was set at rapid fire, which resulted in my gun arching over several targets and a shed firing thirty-eight rounds of ammunition in a few seconds. Everyone froze, followed by a lot of screaming from the range officer. The weapon was taken from me and I was placed in open arrest and escorted back to the Tower and placed in a cell awaiting my fate. I was charged with several serious offences under the Army Act. My commanding officer discovered that I had not received any weapon training and dismissed the charges. I was told to wait outside. Both the training sergeant and his staff were charged with failing to ensure *all* soldiers on the range must have gone through the lectures before. I was called back in and given a special note excusing me from working with weapons. I was now truly a non-combatant, which is what a bandsman should be.

We were now all back at the Tower preparing for our final pass out parade and we had made a considerable improvement from our first day now working together as a smart looking group. My mother sent parcels of food and ten cigarettes each week, which I would share with my roommates; the fruitcake and oatcakes were gone in minutes.

Our final parade arrived, and we marched proudly past the inspecting officer, saluting him with our eyes right after a polished performance of drill without a single mistake. Later in the Mess, Staff Sergeant Siminot met my mother and charmed her as a perfect gentleman, telling her that he had made a man out of me. Pass out parade over, I packed a bag and left with my mother for ten days of leave.

CHAPTER 10

WAITING FOR A POSTING

Returning to the Tower I was given personal interviews to decide my future. I was due to join the band that was presently stationed in Gilgil, Kenya. The Mau Mau, were becoming aggressive and it was decided by my colonel that travel to that area was too dangerous. So, for my safety, I would be kept back at the Tower until the regiment left for the tiny island of Malta, where I would join them three months later for the next posting. Meanwhile I was to become a personal aide to the C.O. and act as his driver and helper. This was a great job for me. I wore civvies most of the time, worked a four-day week and was given complimentary tickets to shows and football games in London. I would finish work by noon most days. No more parades. I began my day making tea for the staff in the orderly room, taking the colonel's wife shopping and safely bringing the sealed password for the Tower to the Queen's house. Ironically most soldiers would get in and out of the Tower in the small hours by using a hidden ladder by the moat and climb up the wall and down into the street. I spent many nights out in London returning at 3:00 using the ladder.

One morning as I was shaving, the soldier next to me began whistling a tune but the melody stayed on one note. He stopped and glanced at me, saying: "Beautiful tune that song isn't it?" Looking at my blank expression he said, "Surely you know 'Around the World in Eighty Days', you're a musician!"

Finally, I received my posting order to Malta, leaving in April. Our training Staff Sergeant Siminot was disliked by most because he would pick on trivial things at room inspection and always demanded more from each recruit. I always tried to be one step in front and I think he respected that and gave me a second chance to prove myself. I suspect the fact that I was a regular soldier and not a national serviceman was the reason for his attitude towards me. He gave me some good advice about joining the band with respect to who could be trusted and who to keep away from. He would be going to Malta at the same time and would keep an eye on me. All troops destined for Malta were kitted out with KD (Khaki Drill), hose tops and puttees. The regiment was flying from Kenya to Malta where we would join them. Travelling to Malta would mean inoculations to prevent disease, which were administered by a lieutenant corporal from the medical corps. I remember looking with horror as I lined up with fifty other soldiers and saw the medic use the same needle on twenty soldiers with men fainting in the line. My turn came and I was given three inoculations: smallpox, yellow fever and one other. My left arm swelled up to twice its size. Staff Sergeant Siminot told me to bump the barrack room floor for an hour and sweat it out. He was right, after forty minutes the swelling went down and I felt better.

I was given a seventy-two-hour pass before leaving for Malta, so I went home to Brighton to say goodbye to family and friends, most of who did not approve of my joining the British Army. I had a vision of what I wanted to have and that was a career in music. Most of my friends had dull, uninteresting jobs working for money with little ambition. *Where was the passion?* My family held a small farewell party on my last Sunday in Brighton. The moment of truth would be Monday morning when I would be on my way to Malta.

CHAPTER 11

MALTA

The island of Malta is 1,300 miles from the United Kingdom and lies almost fifty miles south of Sicily, east of Tunisia and north of Libya. The island is small just sixteen miles long and nine miles wide with signs of religious devotion on every street corner. The capital Valetta is a medieval wall city with Baroque parish churches and painted ceilings. In 1958, the island had a population of approximately 322,000. With Rainy winters and dry, hot summers, H.G. Wells referred to Malta as: "Hells bells, pregnant women and the best collection of rocks I've seen in a lifetime."

23686017 Fusilier M.C.Scholfield in Malta

Our barracks was St Patrick's, situated in Silema, it had been left to our regiment in an awful condition. My first job was unplugging toilets with my hands as I was part of the advance party waiting for the regiment to arrive from Kenya. It would be another two weeks before I was introduced to the band. Routine was very different here to the Tower in the UK. Reveille was at 05:00: wash, shave, and join the breakfast queue. On parade at 06:00 and by noon it would be over one hundred degrees. Our workday was from 06:00 until noon when siesta would begin and there were no more duties for the day. I would wash my KD, hang it on the windowsill and within twenty minutes it would be dry. The entire afternoon would be spent sleeping after preparing our uniforms for the following morning, then supper at 18:00, followed by free time to relax

Straight Street Valetta—known as the 'Gut'—was the red light district of the town. It had a reputation as the seedy underbelly of Valetta. There were plenty of bars with live music and competent piano players. Ladies of the night were working in every bar and entertaining servicemen. Staff Sergeant Siminot introduced me to Maria who, having realised that I was a virgin, was eager to give me lessons.

Having performed my duty, I returned to barracks the following morning completely exhausted. I did not see her again, until she became a good friend of one of the bandsmen and later married him. I believe I had a lucky escape.

Getting back to barracks was a journey in a Gari (horse drawn cart) and was safe and cheap; but travelling by bus was much more entertaining. The bus would come to a stop by each statue of the Virgin Mary and the entire bus would make the sign of the cross, including the driver. This was a different form of Catholicism than I was used to in the UK. I made several trips before the band arrived, finding my way around

Malta, sipping tea at a friendly café in Valetta and enjoying the scenery whilst acquiring a deep tan.

Myself and Brian King in Khaki Drill attire

Peter John Fuller was the bandmaster of the regiment, and was generally disliked by the band. My first impression was that I found him aloof and off hand in his attitude towards me. He asked me what instrument I wanted to play in the band, adding that it could be my choice. Prior to joining the band I could play the piano and violin, so he suggested I try the clarinet, which was not a success. However, I noticed that they had a bassoon in the instrument store, which nobody knew how to play. I began working with this new instrument and made some progress but would not be ready to sit in the band for some time. I was, however, earmarked as a cymbal player for the marching band as the bassoon was not used on the march. In the nearby barracks there was a corporal from the Royal Marines who played bassoon and offered me some free lessons, showing me alternate fingerings and giving me a good supply of reeds. It would be some time before I felt competent enough to sit in a full band. I started working at learning the fingering chart, developing a strong embouchure, practicing my scales, arpeggios, diminished, augmented and dominant progressions, developing a good tone, and working at my intonation to play in tune. After two months of work I sat in a full band practice and was finally accepted.

Bandsmen goofing off

I had been warned about some people in the band who were a bad influence on others, especially newcomers, and to keep my distance. Davy Bonner, who I took an instant liking to, was one of these musicians and we became good friends from the start. Davy had an interesting demeanour and a character to go with it, a heart of gold, free spirit and a great sense of humour. When I first met him he was sitting on top of a locker meditating, but in truth he had just taken some Spanish fly and asked me if I would care for some. He handed me his tea mug and smiled: "Welcome to the band, Mike," he said. "Take a swig." I had no idea what it was, but took a swig. I quickly discovered what Spanish fly was, and its effect on the body, and I walked around feeling amorous for four hours thereafter. Davy played the Tuba, which suited his personality; fun loving, rowdy, nonconformist type with a huge ego, and most of all he was the champion of the underdog. There are many stories involving Davy, which I can share with you, all of them demonstrate his attitude, humour and humility.

Davy Bonner posing as Quasimodo

Ceremonial dress for the band was starched whites, hat, dress cords and a brass sword. It made us feel hot, but we looked smart, nevertheless. Off parade there would be sword fights, all in good fun, but resulted in some swords being broken and a few were reduced to daggers. A visiting general took a closer look on an inspection of the band after he pulled a sword from the scabbard and was left holding a dagger. There was a look of horror on the face of the bandmaster, but the Band Staff Sergeant saved the day by responding: "Is this a dagger I see before me, with the handle toward my hand?"

Under the P. J. Fuller regime, we were often used as a work party for other groups in the regiment, which made our boss popular with both the officers and sergeants. Bandsmen were non-combatant; used as stretcher bearers in the last war, they did not have to go on exercises or run around with rifles. Generally, they were not used for guard duty, hence the expression: "Officers and gentlemen of the band." We would refer to the soldiers as 'squaddies', or G.P.M.G. (general purpose machine gun), pronounced 'Gimpy'.

The band had been assigned (on loan to B Company) to assist in moving lockers and ammunition from a truck and were being yelled at by a young captain complaining that we were to slow. "Can't you band people work any faster?" Davy responded by lifting a large steel locker on his back and running up the stairs, throwing the locker to its designated place. The captain could not believe what he had just seen but there was more to come. Davy took over command, organized us in a chain and began throwing the ammunition boxes from one to the other. The captain began to scream: "Stop! You are handling dynamite and live grenades . . . stop now!" We found the whole situation funny and did manage to slow down a bit, just in case we dropped a box. We were dismissed and marched back to the band room, never to be asked to help again. *Well done, Davy!*

Members of the band were friendly, helpful, good spirited, and it did not take me long to get to know them all. The personnel for a line band allowed by the War Office was thirty-one, which included the bandmaster. But there was a way to have more musicians without actually showing them on strength by attaching them to the band for three months and then select another group to take their place. I am sure the War Office was aware of our plan but this procedure was never questioned or denied.

Looking at a band photo taken in Colchester I was able to place most of their names and bring to mind some of the things they were involved with during their service in London, Malta, North Africa, Colchester and Osnabruck.

There are many stories to be told, all of which hold fond memories for me:

Pipe smoking Brian Edwards was a clarinet player and Dougie Barr was our percussionist. Douglas was a dedicated drummer, who finished up playing professionally for one of the cruise lines is remembered for stealing the flowers from a pub in Osnabruck. Michael Wyness (our timid oboe player who bought a huge car in Germany) can be remembered for his standing up to Tom Leher, who had burst into the dormitory in France very loud and drunk. Not so timid Michael told him to "shut up and go to bed". Tom refused and Michael punched him! Sgt. Brian Smith (our French horn player) wore a glove on his right hand because of an allergy to metal; he suffered a nervous complaint and was finally discharged.

George Hoad (our very competent solo clarinet player) was reputed to plan sexual encounters at 19:30 on a Friday night. George Carr (our excellent euphonium player) was aggressive in nature. He was a friend of Keith Rose (our trombone player), and they both had the shakes from too much beer and finally had to get help. George went out in style after consuming vast amounts of beer stood with his euphonium above his head about to march on at the Berlin Tattoo shouting, "Arrest me, arrest me." He was kicked out of the band for this behaviour and became the regimental post corporal delivering mail.

Peter Radcliffe (our trombone player and artist extraordinaire) drew murals of naked ladies on the wall by everyone's bed space in Tarhuna on our visit to Tripoli. Sgt. Len Hawkins was nicknamed 'stompy', attributed to his playing the trap set and remembered for his performance whilst playing *It ain't going to rain no more* when he successfully lassoed the bandmaster during a performance, hauling him towards the percussion section. Andy Amos (alto saxophone player, jazz fanatic, and anti-establishment) was noted for winning a challenge by drinking half a bottle of gin. Manch Hughes (our tenor saxophone and cohort of Andy), was editor of the band magazine 'Bum note', which contained the monthly news of the band. This was complete with drawings (by Radcliffe), depicting the disgruntled feelings of the bandsmen.

Manch Hughes had great potential and was a constant threat to the establishment. Brian King was our first trumpet player, whose mother bought him an expensive motorbike for his birthday, and was considered to be the richest individual in the band. Dizzy Gillespie presented Errol Ince (our trumpet virtuoso) a golden disc, who joined the band in London taking over the dance band in the first week and transforming the entire group. His playing was wild as was his personal life resulting in his departure finishing as a deserter.

Playing pranks on each other was considered acceptable in the band, regardless of rank, and usually done in good taste without people taking offence. However, this pattern only really got started in Colchester with the arrival of our new Bandmaster Brian Hicks, who not only encouraged this sort of thing but also took part himself. I received a package one morning, which I assumed were new bassoon reeds, but on opening the box I discovered that they were old, dirty and broken. My boss had collected my thrown out reeds and posted them to me although it took me a while to realise that it was my boss. I returned the compliment by arranging for the band to remain silent when his baton came down on the first beat of 'Funicular, Funicular'. Much to his horror I opened a music box with the same tune, but he laughed and accepted my joke.

I remember when someone poured a pint of milk into the tuba bell, which made a low gurgling sound when played and poured out when the water valve was opened. To annoy the trumpet section, a small mint was placed inside the mouth-piece making it impossible to get any note. Playing my bassoon one morning, I noticed that someone had placed a condom on the top, which was inflating as I played. Our Regimental Padre was leaving the regiment, and in his honour he was invited to conduct the band playing his Regimental March 'Trumpet Voluntary'. He arrived for a rehearsal and everything went fine but what he did not realise was that on the evening when he conducted this in front of his fellow officers, Mr. Hicks was playing the solo on a home-made collection of plumbing pipes in front of the band and making some strange sounds. These musicians and others not mentioned would become my family for the next eight years, before I left to study as a student bandmaster in 1966.

In Malta the order of dress was khaki drill, hose tops, puttees and boots for the morning parade. Some mornings the inspecting officer from Headquarter Company would come by the band. He had a lisp and we all would have to really focus not to laugh when he asked: "Any clothing problems Staff Sergeant Sneyd?" whistling with every word beginning with 'S'. The band was part of Headquarter Company and would stand at the back of the parade with instruments for the morning inspection. On one occasion orders were given to go on parade with gasmasks, which not only looked strange but impaired vision and hearing. Major French, OC of Headquarter Company arrived complete with his gasmask; attempting to give the order, he brought the entire company to attention. The scene was hilarious, with soldiers—heads turned—trying to hear the command coming to attention at different times until our illustrious leader took off his mask.

Full band practice was held every morning, which involved going through a series of warm-ups, scales and finally tuning before we were ready to work on any pieces. At noon, siesta was proclaimed, which meant no more work because of the heat. After lunch most of the band would go for a swim in the Mediterranean and having worked from 06:00 to noon, our afternoons were free so we would spend our time sleeping or cleaning our uniforms for the next day. Uniforms were hand washed and then hung on the windowsill, where they would be dry within twenty minutes from the heat of the sun, and then starch ironed.

My marching band instrument was the cymbals, which I was told to take to the R.E.M.E. workshop where someone would buff them until they had a blinding glare. I returned with them and went on parade. We began our first march with a seven-pace roll, but on the fifth crash on my cymbal, the left one flew into the air as the strap chord snapped; the entire band scattered for safety as the cymbal soared above us landing with a deafening crash. My first parade was the subject of conversation for a few weeks but fortunately the cymbal did not hit anyone. There were many entertaining events during my first few months with the fusiliers. Our fearless leader P.J. Fuller used makeup to make his legs look tanned but when he perspired there would be streaks of sweat running down his legs. He was not the bandmaster who defended his band and always had this worried look on his face. In fact, he was disliked to the point where the band played some cruel jokes on him. He had a habit of putting the conductor's baton in his mouth when pondering a measure in the score; the band would grin as he did this and yet he never suspected why we were smirking. At night we would take the batons and stick them into drains and toilets then replace them on the music stand before the morning practice. Later in life as a conductor I always kept my batons in cases and made sure I kept them with me.

CHAPTER 12

MILITARY EXERCISE IN LIBYA

The regiment was leaving for Tripoli, Libya. The band was hoping to remain behind as rear party and look after the camp but unfortunately our commanding officer wanted the band to join them, despite the damage to musical instruments from the sand in the desert. We assembled at the docks in Malta and boarded HMS Striker, a minesweeper where the band was to be in the hull of the ship along with several amphibious vehicles reeking of diesel. Our beds were stretchers, which hooked on to the side of the ship. As we entered the hull with our kit bags and instruments we noticed above us a painting of a huge bear with open arms and underneath was a sign which said: "Abandon hope all ye that enter here". We were now entitled to sea rations and a daily tot of rum. I negotiated a hammock on deck, which was safe in exchange for my rum issue.

The ship's siren rudely awakened me. It was 03:00 and the military exercise was about to begin. I distinctly remember getting dress, grabbing my kit and strapping my bassoon to my back; then up on the rails, I climbed down a scrambling net and then jumped into a beach landing craft, which then rammed the shore. We climbed out and stood in a squad to be inspected. One of the soldiers in B Company was charged for not shaving. Somehow this was not the musical education I had in mind when I joined the Army.

Arriving in Tripoli the temperature was above one hundred degrees and the scene around me was best described as the rich and poor living together in one filthy city. Wafting through my nostrils was the smell of rubbish, sewage and food, and I could hear the sounds of buying and selling from a market close by. The heat was intense; over one hundred degrees at noon and with this temperature you could fry an egg on the pavement. There were two distinct classes here in Tripoli: the very rich and the very poor. I could see a white Mercedes parked by the dock with the chauffeur polishing the bonnet, and not twenty yards from him, a starving horse pulling a heavy load of scrap metal.

Our destination was Tarhunah, a small city south of Tripoli where there was a rundown camp consisting of concrete huts, no windows or doors and a palliasse (a thin straw mattress), for a bed covered by a large mosquito net; although, this was more comfortable than it sounds. Latrines were about one hundred yards away and when used were a good exercise in holding one's breath. Our washrooms were primitive consisting of a large section of corrugated iron shaped into a V with holes for the water pumped in from a pipe above; primitive, but usable. There were bats in the showers which you had to clear out with a wet towel before showering and of course cold water only. The temperature ranged from zero at night to 104 degrees (in the shade) at noon.

The regiment went off on exercise leaving the band as the rear party and were given Stirling guns to guard the camp, but we were issued with blank ammunition! The band gave a concert in the town during which the crowd threw rocks at us; the concert was short lived as a result. A high wire fence separated the camp where the local children would stand outside offering old Roman coins and handmade musical instruments in exchange for clothing. I acquired a musical pipe for a pair of Army pants and a jacket. Later that night it was stolen from my bedside and resold the next day for more clothing. The food was disgusting and the flies usually got to it first, and rather than try to eat in the dining hall, most of us bought cans of soup and beans from the Naafi. Salt tablets were issued for our wellbeing in a hot climate and to augment this we spent our evenings drinking Tenants lager and forming pyramids with the empty cans.

There was an accident involving an APC vehicle (Army Personnel Carrier). While conveying soldiers on an exercise, it rolled over and killed one of the soldiers. I have a vague recollection of someone telling the story of how the remains of the body were swept into a bucket and how the APC had rolled and somersaulted several times. The funeral was held that day with the regimental band in attendance providing the music for the service, which finished rather hurriedly because of an approaching sand storm. The service over, the parade was dismissed. Making our way back to camp, our bass player Davy, reported that he had left his tuba lying in the desert and was driven back to the area in search of his instrument. The tuba was wrapped in a blanket and was found as he had left it but minus the blanket, which demonstrates the value of things in Libya. The blanket was warmth yet only worth a few pennies whereas the tuba was useless but worth considerably more!

We had no TV or radio in North Africa. One day I headed into the town of Tripoli with two friends, and we went to an open roof movie theatre and watched a film entitled 'The Cranes are flying', which was spoken in Russian and had Arabic subtitles. Tripoli was not a safe place to be walking round and we did not stay long finding our way to an American club called Piccolo Capri, where some Americans gave us a lift back to Tarhuna. We had some very entertaining games during our free time and would gather up the sand beetles, which were about the size of small saucers, paint numbers on their backs, place a bet and then race them. There were mornings when we had band practice; I also took a European History class, which gave me my Army First Class certificate towards my education.

I had been in Libya for four weeks and had wished that I was back in Malta. My skin had sores and I had warts on both hands due to the poor sanitation. Then the following week I received news that I had been posted to Knellerhall—the Royal Military School of Music—to study the bassoon for a year. I packed my case, left St Idris Airport in a six-seater military plane to Malta, and boarded a 747, to the UK. Sitting on the plane bound for UK, I noticed people staring at my dark tan, which gave the impression of a six-month holiday in the Mediterranean, which of course, was the case. Arriving at Gatwick, I noticed that my warts had gone, with no trace left on my hands. I was given some disembarkation leave, going home to Brighton before reporting for duty at Knellerhall.

CHAPTER 13

THE ROYAL MILITARY SCHOOL OF MUSIC – KNELLERHALL

Knellerhall, the Royal Military School of Music, named after Sir Godfrey Kneller, has been the home of Army music since 1857. The school is situated in the town of Whitton close to the Twickenham rugby ground and not far from the town of Richmond with The Duke of Cambridge (pub) opposite the main gates. It was the Duke who was responsible for forming the RMSM. This came after an embarrassing performance of British Army Bands playing 'God Save the Queen' simultaneously in different pitches, arrangements and key signatures, resulting in humiliation!

My stay in 1959 was a memorable one, which allowed me the opportunity to study. I had lessons from professional teachers: Frank Rendell for bassoon; Mr. Jones for violin, and

Mr. Tulip for piano. Both Rendell and Jones played in the London Philharmonic Orchestra, and Mr. Tulip was a retired bandmaster. My bassoon needed some major repairs and was sent away to a factory in Manchester and I was given a French bassoon (the buffet system), which was different to my Monig (German fingering). I set about the task of learning the new fingering and got off to a slow start. Piano lessons were held in the back room of a café in the high street with Mr. Tulip teaching piano and his son serving tea, toast and bacon butties in the front room.

Our working days were busy with many activities; morning room inspections, parades, lessons, group practice, Company Band and Full Band. We were billeted eight pupils to a room, and within the week we got to know one another, each from a different regiment. Evenings were free for us to discover the local pubs in Twickenham and Richmond, returning late and ready for bed and to face another long day playing music. Each morning began with a room inspection and each room had a student bandmaster assigned to its care. Student Al Briggs was our fearless leader, and after the room inspection, he would throw his overcoat on a bed and pick it up at the end of the day. One day one of my pupil comrades had taken the time to stitch his coat to the bed. Briggs came to pick up his coat and he dragged his coat and blankets towards the door. Everyone howled with laughter, including Student Briggs: "Okay, I've got the message."

One morning there was a pupil in a bed near me, who did not get up. He seemed tired and weak, and refused to move even after some shouting from the RSM. Eventually the Medical Officer was summoned who, after examining him, called for an ambulance. It came to our attention that he was suffering from "extreme fatigue". His best friend commented: "When you're out shagging every night, what do you expect, the body needs rest to re-charge the batteries," to which we all agreed.

Wednesday evening was concert night and the school had to be prepared for thousands of visitors. Pupils were assigned various duties: setting out chairs, marking car parks and handing out programmes. If it was a grand concert with 1812 on the programme, there would be firework duty. This was a lot of fun; setting off smoke grenades and throwing a thunder flash at the correct time hoping that it would explode on not only the correct measure but on the exact beat of the bar. It was a complex formula; lighting the thunder flash, holding it for at least eight seconds, then running away and throwing it away from the back of the bandstand during the next seven seconds, before it exploded. A senior student would be reading the music score shouting out instructions of when to light, run and throw.

Six years later on my return to Knellerhall as a student, I was given the opportunity as chief of fireworks and intending to make my mark as a future bandmaster. This was my final concert before leaving and remembered that the Director of Music, Lieutenant Colonel Basil Browne, had previously complained about there not being enough smoke during the battle scene. I ordered my team to place *all* the smoke canisters on the corrugated metal sheets to give a better effect, not realising that I had used a complete year's supply. The result was truly amazing as the smoke billowed up and around the bandstand, enveloping the entire massed band of 200 with Basil Browne disappearing from view, followed by the audience. After the concert—feeling certain I was in trouble—the Director summoned me. Carrying a big grin on his face, he shook my hand and congratulated me on my (smoke) performance, saying: "Well done, Mr. Scholfield, the best smoke effect I have ever witnessed. How many cans did you use?"

I replied: "Just a few extra, sir."

Returning to my pupil days, I was on chair duty hauling chairs from the main building to the concert area and one of the comments made by a fellow pupil was, "I bet we'll be dragging bloody chairs fifty years from now!" How true that statement was!

One Wednesday I was assigned to meet a group of blind people, some in wheel chairs and usher them to the front of the bandstand. I was to meet them at Whitton Station; meeting with the RSM I asked: "How will they be able to see me at the station if they are blind?"

The RSM shouted, "Don't be bloody silly, they will have someone with them who can see!" I had several other encounters with the RSM, Sam Lowe. One of which was when I was returning from a duty as a night guard and I had to report to the RSM with details of the twenty-four-hour guard. All was in order, with the exception of a bed sheet that had gone missing. As I began to report this, I was stopped mid-sentence and told that I could not discuss sheets at this desk and was told to move to another desk two feet to my right. The RSM explained that this was the desk to report missing sheets. This was typical of the Army mentality.

Every Friday afternoon was a cross-country run, about four miles with a route planned with three locations where the runner collected a ticket. My plan with three other pupils was to visit each location in a different order, steal a ticket from each and then go for a cup of tea in the Whitton café and still arrive near the end having escaped the gruelling run. The plan worked for six weeks but on the next run I got caught stealing a ticket at the second location and was marched in front of the RSM, who demanded to know who my accomplices were. Of course, loyalty was of great importance and I denied that other pupils were involved. My punishment was three extra weekends working in the kitchen scrubbing pots and pans. I did, however, end up sharing those the duties with my partners in crime.

Each Friday the school would go on parade at 16:00. We had to collect six pieces of rubbish to be granted dismissal, but to save time, most of us wore our civilian clothes under our denim uniform. We looked huge with our civvies under our working order but it worked. Once the parade was over, we rushed to our rooms, ripped off our denims, and then ran down to the high street to Whitton Station and go our separate ways for the weekend. I spent most of my weekends in Brighton staying with my parents and visiting a girl named

Marion, who I had met at my brother's wedding, and who later became my wife.

A fellow bassoon player from the Royal Signals had a Lambretta—a small scooter—, which we would use to travel to Brighton. We would party at the Regent ballroom and then attempt to get back to Whitton. Driving back very slowly at 03:00 one Monday morning, I fell off the back of the scooter, tore my trousers and grazed my knee. On this particular weekend there had been a brutal murder in a back alley close to the school of music, and all musicians were grounded and interviewed. My trousers were taken to a forensic laboratory to check for matching blood. The police were sure that whoever committed the crime was from Knellerhall; yet, after detaining 200 musicians for two days, the police decided to look elsewhere and eventually found the two men responsible for this ghastly crime. During my year at the school, I made many friends, shared a lot of music, played in small string and woodwind groups, full band, orchestra, and had private lessons from the finest professors.

CHAPTER 14

BACK TO THE TOWER

By faith I was an Anglican marrying a Roman Catholic, and had to take some Catholic instruction in London. The priest who had been assigned to me was at least ninety years old, greeted me at the door of the rectory with his soft Irish brogue. When I told him I played the organ, he skipped the instruction and asked me to play for him. I turned up each Tuesday for the next six weeks and played the organ. One evening I was playing and I happened to look in my mirror and I noticed some activity in the church. Several nuns were walking towards the altar and lighting candles, followed by a long silence. A priest arrived and was looking up at me, waiting for me to begin the service for that evening. I had no music, and was also totally clueless as to the order of service. The door to the organ loft opened, and in rushed the organist for that day: "Sorry

I'm a bit late," he whispered as he pushed me off the organ bench. I returned each Tuesday evening to practice the organ, checking first that there was not a service, and continued my Catholic instruction.

My mother-in-law to be, persuaded me to get married in uniform in a Catholic church in Brighton. I was just nineteen years old, and my wife was seventeen. Our Honeymoon was in Torquay at a hotel similar to 'Fawlty Towers', and looking back now, we were both too young for marriage, rushing into it without getting to know one another first. As a newly married couple, we were put on a waiting list for accommodation; my wife stayed with her parents, and I would travel back and forth from Brighton to the Tower, where the regiment had returned from Malta. Our band sergeant Nick Sneyd was an experienced musician, excellent Eb clarinet player who could sight-read anything placed in front of him. He was also in charge of discipline of the band. So, when I missed the train and returned late from leave, he charged me with no excuses accepted, handing me three days' restriction of privileges. This would mean working in the kitchen and cleaning toilets, reporting in my best uniform for the staff parade at 10:00 and inspected by the Orderly Officer. I learnt my lesson and I was never late on parade again.

(In present days—some sixty-five years later—discipline appears scared to raise its head and correct the young with society, substituting compromise in its place; having spent time here in Canada teaching in schools it seemed the norm never to fail a student or give a really low mark. I taught some university students an Edmus100 class in La Ronge, Saskatchewan, and was told to higher the marks by the Dean, as my marking did not fit the Bell curve. This was nonsense to give false hope to students who needed to work harder, and therefore learn from the experience. My highest mark in school was seventy-five in English Literature, and only a high mark of one hundred in Music Aural tests, whereas I hear of students being awarded high nineties in most subjects at school nowadays.)

CHAPTER 15

ROYAL FUSILIERS POSTING TO COLCHESTER 1959

After only three weeks of arriving in Colchester I found a rented house available and my wife and I moved in to this small hiring only a short distance away from the barracks. The house was damp needing a lot of work with draughty windows, mould in most of the rooms, and overall it was not a healthy place. Still, the rent was all I could afford, so I would have to wait until my name was at the top of the married quarter's list or find a better place to live.

Concert band at Colchester

I was offered a bike from a major in the regiment, which had belonged to his wife and snapped up the deal. I did not mind that it was a ladies' bike with no crossbar, so I gave the major a cheque for three pounds. On my regular journey to barracks from home one day I noticed a police car following me, but not stopping. The third time this happened I stopped and spoke with the policeman, and asked, "Why are you following me? Can I help you with something?"

The policeman replied: "Don't be cheeky with me, soldier. We know the bike is stolen." He then called me a "bloody thief".

I replied: "I'm going to report you." At no time was I asked to prove ownership. Later I found the cancelled cheque in my wallet, which I would have shown him but he had assumed a soldier riding a ladies' bike in Colchester had to be stolen. I rode my bike with him following slowly behind me in his car to the police station and asked to speak to the superintendent. I was kept waiting for a long time and phoned my father in London, who gave me the name of a good lawyer. Finally, I was ushered into an office and after I had proved my claim of ownership, mentioned the name of my lawyer; I received an apology from both the chief inspector and the policeman.

Our new band room was state of the art; complete with a high ceiling, musical notes on the floor, but no coat hooks and it seemed that modern architecture had missed some of the essentials. There was a light high up in the middle, which gave poor lighting for the band and could only be reached to change the bulb with an extension ladder. The instrument store had insufficient shelving as it was just too small, but our library was a good size for our huge selection of music. The library was in alphabetical order, stored in sturdy cases for travelling and could be set up anywhere within thirty minutes. The scores were in linen jackets clearly marked with a number, regularly inspected for damage by Sergeant Smith our librarian and his six assistants. Several libraries of this kind were auctioned when some bands disbanded in the eighties for $30.000 or more.

Within a year of moving to Colchester, we had an invasion of bugs that were eating the music paper and had to call a specialist to deal with this problem, as these tiny insects were systematically destroying our library. An entomologist was called who placed an insect bomb in the room, sealed all windows and doors, leading a fuse outside the room and set it in motion. The fuse was lit and on returning the following morning the room was ankle deep with insects and our library saved. Band rehearsals carried on but there seemed to be a lot of tension surrounding bandmaster P. J. Fuller. The phone rang incessantly from the office beside the practice room, with our bandmaster rushing away to take the calls. I asked the Band Sergeant Nick Sneyd what was going on, but his lips were sealed and just smiled, shaking his head and saying, "You will find out soon enough."

Tuba section, Davy Bonner and Harry Lawrence

Royal Fusiliers Band – Colchester

At one rehearsal the bandmaster suddenly remembered that the band were due to play at the Officers' Mess that night and, although he was sorry about the short notice, we were ordered, not invited to attend.

That memorable evening turned out with most of the band drunk, with silly grins on our faces after an afternoon of drinking in the Naafi to show our disapproval. That night our music was full of mistakes with wrong notes, missing key signatures and playing too loud. The band always played in a separate room and could be heard but not seen. At the close of the evening the officers would gather around the band for the traditional playing of regimental marches in order of seniority. We began to play the first march and could see the look of horror on the face of the adjutant who was a musician and realised that there was something seriously wrong with our rendition. The crowning glory came when we played our final march, which was our own (Fighting with the seventh Fusiliers) part of which had 'Rule Britannia', where the band stood up in sections at different times. We had bandsmen standing at the wrong time roaring with laughter, sitting down, and then getting it wrong a second time much to the look of horror on the bandmaster's face; but there was nothing he could do to save the day. Our colonel stood there, shame faced and his moustache drooping, while some of the junior officers were roaring with laughter. The band were charged, cautioned, and then forgiven when the truth was revealed about that day and the questionable career prospects of our bandmaster.

Band and Drums en route to an engagement

Saxophones and Bassoon practice

We did not see our bandmaster for a while; he was either away looking at future places for the band to play at, or was he too embarrassed to appear. There was something definitely wrong but nobody said anything, although there were rumours that our boss was in trouble with money. He had been "cooking the books", robbing Peter to pay Paul. He had been living beyond his means, borrowing money and then finding it hard to pay everyone back. On one occasion I was going to London the day before payday to set things up for a band tour and he suggested that he would collect my pay on my behalf and give it to me later in London when the band arrived. It was a week before I received my pay and I knew then that he was in serious trouble and would not be with us much longer.

On returning to Colchester we had a sub-bandmaster, Mr. Thompson from Knellerhall to run the band. He was an experienced conductor and had a wicked sense of humour. When the music was wrong, his favourite expression was: "By the fucking left!" and in contrast to another director, bandmaster plumber, who would stop the band after a mistake and say, "T'was ever thus, for forty years they wandered." During a rehearsal one morning, our new director looked out the window, saw that the sky was cloudy, put down the baton and announced, "I'm off fishing, see you all tomorrow."

A full-scale investigation began, with every musician being interviewed by the Criminal Investigation Branch, building his or her case against our bandmaster. I recall that all monies that he had borrowed from various funds had been repaid, however, his behaviour was unacceptable to the investigation, which seemed unfair. Our bandmaster P.J. Fuller was court martialled later that month, charged and dismissed with ignominy, facing life with a criminal record. I can remember him returning to K.H. some years later in search of a pardon, which I believe he was never granted and was last heard of running a pub in the town of Bude in Cornwall.

We now awaited the arrival of a new bandmaster Brian Hicks, who I had met previously at K.H. on my pupil's course in 1959. Promotion is slow in a band but soon after his arrival I was promoted with the rank of Lance Corporal and my new responsibilities were to work as band office clerk, which would involve coping with the paperwork, oversee and organize all things for the engagement season. I would organize transport for the band and keep records of enrolment, postings and transfers. In addition to this, I played bassoon in the concert band, baritone saxophone, or bass drum in the marching band and piano for the dance band.

One of the transfers into the band was a tuba player named Corporal Harry Lawrence from the band of the Horse Guards. He was a seasoned player, complete with a scar on his lip, which he acquired when his horse reared in fright after someone threw a firework at the feet of the horse. The tuba mouthpiece cut his lip and broke some teeth but he survived and seemed to be a better player despite the setback. Davy— our loan tuba player—particularly welcomed his arrival, allowing him to take a rest during the music plus getting some moral support in the tuba section. The band were rehearsing one hot afternoon without Davy, who was missing, but finally appeared wearing a raincoat. He was ushered into the rehearsal but refused to take off his coat, so he was taken to the office where he finally removed it to show that he had a long slide from the tuba wedged on his hand, which was swollen from attempts to remove it. Poor Davy was so embarrassed but did see the funny side to his predicament, only after the slide was removed at the medical centre.

It was at this time that I realized I needed to buy my first car, but first I had to pass my driving test. I passed the test the following month in an Army Jeep and started looking for a second-hand vehicle to spend the fifty pounds my grandfather had left me in his will. I saw a car advertised for sale in Brighton, which had been parked in a garage for a year and the owner—a lady who was getting married and selling the car to pay for her wedding—only wanted thirty-seven pounds for the car. It turned out that my insurance was only twenty pounds, which was just over half the purchase price of the car. It was a red 1935 MG, which had been raced some years before and was a P.G. series with a leather belt around the bonnet, twin carburettors, crank start, spoke wheels, and cable brakes. The petrol tank was at the rear and the windshield could be wound down for racing. The cable brakes were sensitive and it took three attempts before my car passed the road test. My brother was going to drive my car from Brighton to Colchester but the car broke down in London on its way to Colchester with a broken half shaft. I had to hunt round to find one but finally had the car repaired and collected it the following week driving to Colchester.

I received news that better quarters were available for me and my wife,my wife, and me and we could move the next week to a large maisonette, the ground floor of a mansion.

One flight up was the owner's residence, separate from ours, who was a retired sea commodore, and both he and his wife were friendly and helpful.

My wife was pregnant and we would soon be expecting our first child. Opposite our new home was a nurse's residence, and I arranged for Marion to have the baby at home with a midwife from the residence in attendance. Clive was born at home on the 9 December 1961. In the following months, Clive cried at night, and we coped as best we could as new parents. Some nights I would place him in the carrycot and take him for a car ride, to help him sleep. After several weeks of his crying I took him to a nurse, who dismissed my concerns, but later it transpired that Clive had a perforated eardrum; no wonder he was crying.

One afternoon, I was walking down the street carrying my bassoon when I met a man trimming the hedge in his front garden. He asked what was in my case: "A bassoon," I replied.

"Just what we need," he said. He was a member of a musical group, who was planning to practice the Schubert octet, and they were looking for a bassoon player.

A week later I joined the group, practising for the whole year on a Wednesday evening in an old tailor's shop on the high street. One Sunday the group came to my rented house, which had a huge drawing room and French doors overlooking an expansive lawn. There was a wisteria creeper hanging by the doors, which gave a perfumed smell to the room, making it a perfect setting for playing music. The Schubert octet required, first and second violins, viola, cello, double bass, French horn, clarinet and bassoon. Playing chamber music of this difficulty was a lot of fun and also challenging for all of us, but after a lot of serious practises, we gave our first, and only performance, to a group of elderly people in a care home.

CHAPTER 16

COMMUNITY ORCHESTRA

At this time I joined a Community Orchestra at the University of Colchester, where I met the eccentric conductor Dr. Spinx. Sat in the orchestra for the first time, Dr. Spinx stopped conducting and pointed at me, saying: "Are you new? What's your name?" Later that month he asked me if I would like a private piano lesson. My colleagues told me that I should feel privileged to be asked, and there would be no charge for the lesson; he selected students who he thought would benefit from his knowledge. He had a PhD in piano performance, played harpsichord on BBC 3, and was married to a Spanish concert pianist. I accepted his invitation for a lesson on improvisation. He would pick me up at 08:15, drive to his house in Suffolk, which was an old barn converted into a beautiful home with two grand pianos.

As we journeyed, he explained how the lesson would proceed. I was to create a melody for a few measures, then expand the theme, improvising and moving through several keys and then return to the first idea. After meeting his wife, I sat at the piano, whilst he went to the bathroom to shave, shouting out comments as I played: "Michael, key of G this beautiful morning, get playing, spread your wings, be creative!" I must have played for about fifteen minutes, when suddenly he was by my side. He pushed me from the piano stool and proceeded to play exactly what I had just played. He saw my look of astonishment and said, "What's the matter, Michael. Surely you can do this, can't you?" He was a brilliant musician. I could not have performed as he had. He then suggested different pivots and chords in my theme, and also showed me alternative ways of key changing; some of them were very subtle. The first part of my lesson ended at noon, followed by picking up some fresh meat from the butcher's shop in the village, and returning home where his wife cooked a tasty lunch of steak (cooked on coals). My lesson resumed, learning about improvisation until 17.00, I learned more that day than from any piano lesson I had been given before. On our way home, Dr. Spinx advised me to leave the Army, study for my A.R.C.M. at the university, and join his staff. He seemed shocked to find out that I was married and had a young son, "Too young," he retorted, and perhaps he was right. My life would have been very different if I had taken that step, however, I decided to remain with the Army band.

I continued playing in the orchestra, getting ready for a Christmas performance, when Dr. Spinx—forgetting a score at home—asked me to take his car to get the music. I could only get into his car by climbing in the passenger side, and I discovered there was a large hole in the floor with a tree trunk lying on the back seat. He told me this was the hand break, and used it when parking on hills; however, I managed to bring back the music without incident, despite his dangerous car. His eccentricity was endless, coming to conduct a concert one evening with only the right side of his face shaved, giving the explanation that he was running late. Ear training lessons from him were certainly different, with all spoken words sung, no talking was permitted, and even students coming into the library had to sing. It was hilarious; as students approached the library they were asked to sing, but then decided that they no longer wanted a book, as they were not going to sing.

During an ear training session one afternoon, a motorcycle roared past the window. On its return, Dr. Spinx threw a chair out the window, yelling at the motorcyclist. Fortunately, he missed.

My last encounter with Dr. Spinx was in a classroom with fifteen new music students who had enrolled to take a Diploma study course for the London College of Music. After his welcome, he then asked the group, who played the piano? Nine of the students were unable to play the piano, so he dismissed them saying: "Get your money back, take some piano lessons and then come back in a year!" The students were in shock, but having left, some of them took his advice.

CHAPTER 17

BAND ENGAGEMENTS

The arrival of our new bandmaster was a pleasant change from the previous director. Mr. Hicks was an excellent musician, played the French horn, a good conductor, but most of all he had a great sense of humour. The band started to improve; our repertoire expanded and playing in full band was a pleasure. The concert season was busy with engagements as far as the West Country, being hired to play for the Lynton Lynmouth remembrance service, where the town was flooded in 1952, killing thirty-four people and leaving 400 people homeless. It was rumoured that the cause was man-made (rain making, by seeding selected clouds).

These were experiments that took place in the early 1950s, but it was claimed that these exercises were conducted in secret. However, the storm, which caused the 1952 disaster, was not confined to the Lynmouth area, with heavy rain falling over the West Country and South Wales. The storm depression was several hundred miles across, and in reality was not the result of cloud seeding experiments. The town celebrates each year with a Thanksgiving ceremony, hiring a band to present a concert for this event.

One of the bigger engagements was the West Country Agriculture show, which the band would perform over a five-day period. We had breaks between the three concerts each day, and with the weather becoming uncomfortably hot, I fell asleep in the sun for two hours and got sunstroke. I spent one day lying in the First Aid tent, flirting with a nurse who was placing cold towels on my face to stop the fever, as I listened to our band. We were the guest band for other functions, including a concert for the Officers' Mess in a remote town in Devon. The band had been drinking western ales, which were stronger than most, causing everyone to fart continually throughout the concert. After a smoke break, our bandmaster appeared at the end of the passage leading to the band area. He raised his arms for us to begin playing, but we could not stop laughing as he had tied a scarf round his head because of the smell.

Returning to Colchester we began working hard on our concert music in preparation for an important audition. Army bands were selected by Sir Harry Mortimer to play live music for 'Music While You Work' show. We were accepted and went to London giving a live performance on the BBC Home Service Basic, 22 May 1963. The morale in the band had changed now to a very positive one. Our standard of playing had improved, and as a result, we were in demand to play at functions involving marching, dance and concert bands. Our repertoire had changed, with some challenging music given to the band, solos for each section, chamber music and for the first time a choral group was encouraged. I was given the bassoon solo *Lucy Long*, a piece of four movements, telling the story of Lucy, who goes to a dance, has too much to drink, feels light headed (third movement), then sobers up and runs all the way home. On one occasion with this piece on the programme, I was standing having a pee in the Gents' washroom when my last reed fell from my mouth into the urinal. However, I retrieved it, and then washed the reed before returning it to my mouth. My bandmaster announced my solo and added: "Note the urinal tone."

Just prior to Mr. Hicks arriving, I had applied for a position as an organist at SHAPE headquarters in Brussels. The requirement was for a musician from the Fusilier Brigade who was able to play piano and organ for services. I did not receive an answer, but was told by my Band Sergeant that P.J. Fuller, who wanted my musical ability for the Fusilier Band, had no intention of forwarding my application for the position, and had placed it in his desk.

Posting orders came through with news that our next home would be in Osnabruck, North Rhine in West Germany, with three months to get organized, debts paid, cars sold, and pack up our goods and chattels. This would be an unaccompanied posting to begin with; our families would join us later, after we had found a place to live. Most of us in the band did not have enough seniority to qualify for an Army Quarter, and again my wife and son moved back with her mother until I could find a suitable place for us to live.

CHAPTER 18

OSNABRUCK 1963–1966

Our next posting was Osnabruck, North Rhine, West Phalia, which was not the friendliest part of Germany. We had been told that the local people were cold; they were mostly Roman Catholic and, as a result of the Second World War, anti-British. Barely twenty years had passed since WWII, and the bitterness was still evident on both sides.

The waiting list for a quarter was long, and as a young soldier with junior rank, I was at the bottom end of the list. Determined to find us somewhere to live, I began to learn how to speak German so I could converse with the local people. Public relations were a big part of the forces' plan, with the band playing a major part in improving the situation between the Germans and the British, performing at local festivals and marching band displays.

My first attempt at trying to speak German turned out to be an interesting experience. I had a phrase book, and had already looked at some of the important phrases I would need to at least get by; hopefully, by making an effort to speak German, I would be appreciated. Four of us decided we should explore our new area, by opening a map, sticking a pin in the middle, and that would be our choice. The town indicated was called Rheine, some thirty kilometres west of Osnabruck. We changed into civilian clothes, but by our short hair and our heavy British accent, everyone would guess that we were soldiers. I came prepared, and had already mastered the phrase: "Excuse me, where is the station." ("Entschuldigen sie bitte, wo ist der Bahnhof?") We met some people coming towards us, so I tried to speak some German. They smiled, but had understood my question and gave us directions in German, which none of us understood accept the direction they pointed. We walked for another ten minutes, and beginning to doubt, I asked again and was pointed in the opposite direction. Finally, the impressive station came in view. We joined a queue, which gave me time to practice my German. "Four tickets to Rheine please." I arrived at the ticket window and said: "Vier stuck für Rheine, bitte."

The man at the ticket office replied: "'hullo, mate, you get your tickets over there," pointing to another queue, "this is a post office!" We collapsed with laughter, and changed queues. *Maybe I should not try any more German, or let someone else have a go*, I thought. We finally got our tickets and had some time for a few beers, before we boarded our train.

The journey to Rheine was twenty minutes, and we left the station and found a Gasthaus. The food in most German pubs was excellent, Bratwurst, Bochwurst, or frigadella (cold pork chop with mustard) washed down with a cold beer; this was good living. We left and wandered towards the riverbank. The weather was mild, the sun was shining and we lay down on the bank, relaxing, falling asleep until we were startled by the sound of people near us. There was a huge picnic beside us with about a hundred people, and we were invited to join them, drinking more beer of course. The Germans like to party and they like their beer. We returned later that evening, and all agreed that the local folk seemed friendly and this had the makings of a good posting. We had a full week of orientation, lectures and films about Osnabruck, including places that were out of bounds, and the location of the Green Howard regiment in the same town. We began to organize our band practice room, which was situated on the top floor of a barrack block. We set up the music library, which was in wooden crates and ready to use in alphabetical order, while selecting a suitable room for a social club and then begin decorating.

My main concern now was to find some suitable accommodation for my family, who were still in the UK. This would not be an easy task, and one that would be made more difficult because of the language barrier. I had no luck for the first three months, until a trombone player from the band told me that he had met a German girl called Hanna-Laura, who was bilingual and she would help me find a place for my family. I would get her to translate the ads from the local paper, then together we would visit the flats and she would negotiate with the owner on my behalf.

On our fourth attempt, we found a two-bedroom apartment, situated two miles from the camp. The owner was a widow and her late husband had been a major in the SS. The apartment was fully furnished, with reasonable rent, and getting the Army housing officer to inspect, I was given permission to sign the lease. Later in the apartment, I found a lot of personal items belonging to the owner's late husband; after discussing this with Hanna-Laura, I was told that the owner had no interest in keeping any of this. Clearing out a desk, I found medal ribbons and a gold swastika, which I later gave to one of my sons. I phoned my wife with the good news about the apartment and my family arrived a month later in Osnabruck.

Settling in our new apartment and learning the German customs, we soon developed into a routine, which included an understanding of the dustbin-system and parking. Recycling started in the 1960s in Germany, some thirty years ahead of most countries, with heavy fines for non-compliance.

One morning my wife was feeling really sick; not able to get out of bed and without a telephone, I went to get help but collapsed on the bus. Later, we were told that we both had food poisoning, which had come from eating fresh cream cakes from across the street. My only means of transport was by bus, and it was time to buy a second-hand car.

I found a black Simca at the right price, read up on the German Highway Code, passed the test and attached my

BFG plates; finally, I had wheels. We received notice that the apartment was up for sale, but the owner offered us a new flat nearer the barracks, which we gladly accepted. Moving again but this time it was a little easier with my own transport.

With our second child on the way, my wife was overdue and was feeling tired and anxious about the birth. She took some castor oil to speed things up, however, I believe she took a little too much as the next at morning, at 02:00, 27 January 1964, Malcolm arrived in our bedroom. I wrapped him in my shirt, checked that he was okay and then phoned the doctor. An ambulance arrived and took mother and child to a German hospital and later transferred them to a British Military Hospital, where Malcolm and his mother rested for a few days.

Within the next year the band had established its reputation, and were accepting engagements in Denmark; with our first visit to Copenhagen, we stayed at the Life Guard barracks. My job in the band office was to arrange the transport, and confirm accommodation for the band. We would cross the border into Denmark and required the correct paperwork to pass through the Danish customs with our bus. We gave several concerts at the Tivoli gardens, which were successful and returned on two more visits. The band had discovered that the Danes wanted our cigarettes and booze, which we could buy (duty free) and sell at a profit. On our next visit to Copenhagen, the band set up shop in the barracks and everyone made a substantial profit, although our actions were illegal, and later we would pay the price of smuggling.

The following year the band was invited to Heidelberg in southern Germany, staying with the 280th American Army group, who made us most welcome. My rank was now Corporal and had started to get a bit more pay for my work, but more responsibility was expected from me having to discipline the younger musicians in the band. We gave marching displays for the Americans who liked our old-fashioned way of marching. Our hosts took the band to see the castle in Heidelberg and a visit to the concentration camp at Dachau. What we saw at this dreadful place was unimaginable! Gas ovens, showers (with large holes for the gas), blood ditches, where people were gunned down and then covered with quick lime, hooks with wire for hanging, and the unliveable quarters with bunk beds. As we visited there was a silence, which continued throughout the bus journey back to the barracks. Looking back now over the years I still find it hard to imagine what it must have been like to be subjected to this barbaric behaviour.

On this particular visit several members of the band had used their private vehicles to make the journey. We had driven from Osnabruck to Heidelberg, and upon arrival were booked to play at an American club for a four-hour dance, with only a couple of hours rest before we played. The band played for the first hour without any problem but we were exhausted and were having trouble to stay awake. The bouncer of the club, came up to me and said, "Take one of these, this will put you right," and within ten minutes I was wide-awake, had an energy surge, but did not realize what I had taken. The bouncer then gave the same pill to the rest of the band.

We had been given a 'Benny', commonly known as an 'upper', which gave a high for a few hours, followed by the body catching up later. A lesson well learnt, *not to take pills from strangers*! Although, I must admit it worked.

Returning to Osnabruck, we had managed to acquire two sousaphones, complete with detachable bells and two sturdy cases to store them. I believe that we were the first British Military Band to go on parade with sousaphones. The American Army issues musical instruments to their bands, having a life of three years and are then auctioned off to the highest bidder. Our bandmaster had bid on the sousaphones, acquiring them for one hundred dollars each.

Having changed my Simca for a new Mini, another year had passed by and my wife was pregnant with our third child. We were granted a married quarter just in time for the arrival of our daughter Julia Denise, who was born on 28 October 1965.

Denmark was the favourite country for the band to visit; Copenhagen was followed by five more engagements in the small town of Varde, 300 kilometres west of Copenhagen, and with a population 13,000. The band fell in love with this little town and they fell in love with us. After our third visit, most of the band had somewhere to stay. We were made 'Freemen' of the city, and given a card at a civic ceremony by the mayor of Varde. Inside the card it was inscribed: "As a generous token you shall have the right to one free beer a day as long as you live – on your visit in Varde 1965," and by the time of our last visit, we no longer required lodgings; everyone had somewhere to stay. The Danish people were very hospitable; many of the musicians had girlfriends, with three band members later marrying Danish girls. There were many good stories, involving hospitable Danes.

On one particular visit we decided to take one of the cannon balls from the front of the Danish Life Guard barracks. We really wanted this a trophy for our band room in Osnabruck. Our plan was successful. Nobody seemed to spot the missing cannon ball. On a return visit, we had planned to take another one to match the cannon ball in Osnabruck. We placed the cannon ball in the suitcase of the new recruit to the band, but he was caught and tried to explain. Both Corporal Jim Dott and I confessed, ready to face the music. To our amazement, the Commandant smiled and told us that we only had to ask and we would have been given as many as we wanted. There was a supply of several hundred.

After a concert in Varde, I went for a beer with Cpl Jim Dott. I tried ordering in German, but the barman ignored me. Later, speaking English, we finally got served. The barman apologised, adding: "We don't serve Germans here." As the evening progressed, we noticed a man having difficulty getting up from his table; his wife was trying to help him up, but he was too heavy. We went to help, and finally got him home while his wife drove. We carried him up a flight of steps to his flat, and then got him to bed. She asked our names and where we were staying, and ordered a taxi for us to get back to barracks. The following day we were free until 19:00, when we had another concert. We received a message from a chauffeur who was waiting outside our barrack block; we had been invited to have drinks with the man we helped the previous evening. He was the Captain of a Danish frigate, which was alongside the harbour. We changed into our concert uniform and ran down to the waiting car. Arriving at the frigate, we were piped on board, past the crew of the ship, and seated at the Captain's table. Above the table was a cord, which he pulled and three Carlsberg arrived. We were drinking Elephants' Carlsberg, strong, like the elephant, in both flavour and alcohol content (7.2%). We were given a variety of cheese and meats, and the beer kept coming. I could see that things could get out of hand and that we had to remain sober for the concert. The beer cord was pulled for the last time as our host sensed our predicament and said that he would personally deliver us safely to our band, his chauffeur driving of course. On arrival at the barracks, the band was waiting. Word had already gone out to our band-master where we had gone, however, we were not late. Our Captain shook hands with our bandmaster who smiled and said, "One wrong note from either of you, and you will forfeit your pay!"

We passed the test.

Our visits to Varde were all marked with good memories. The sponsor for the Ringrider fest was a Mr. Johanson, who owned a travel agent business and co-owned a fashion model-ling company with his wife. Some of the band had been invited to lunch with him and his wife. At the table he asked his wife how much money she had with her. She opened her handbag and replied: "About 4,000 kroner." He said that this was not going to be enough for them to fly to Spain for a fashion show and pay the wages for the models. In the 1960s, most people used cash. He called for a courier to go to the bank and bring a few more thousand kroner for their trip. After this incident I began to wonder just how well off this couple were; later that evening we found out. There were ten of us visiting with Mr. Johanson late in the evening and the owner of the bar, called for last orders. Johanson called out: "You can't close the bar when our English guests are enjoying our hospitality. I'll buy this place from you, to keep it open. How much do you want for it?" A figure was agreed, and Johansen wrote out a cheque for the agreed amount and we could not believe our eyes and ears but later we wondered if this whole stunt had been staged for our benefit. The cheque was torn up the following day, but if presented, would have been honoured. We now knew that he was a millionaire but tragically he died one year later from alcohol poisoning leaving a fortune to his widow.

On our last visit to Denmark, I drove ahead in my car to clear the paperwork for our visit, and had got to know the customs officials through our many visits. I was told to warn the band that there would be a check for cigarettes and liquor on the bus. Someone in Denmark, who had been charged too much for a bottle of scotch, had reported to the customs that the band was selling cigarettes and booze to the Danes illegally. If the band declared everything at the border, it could be collected on the return journey without charge. I drove back to meet the bus and delivered my message, but nobody believed me. They took a chance, and as a result, all the contraband was taken from the bus and confiscated. The news made the local

Osnabruck, and National papers. The heading was 'Band with Contraband'. We were in disgrace, and the talk of the regiment for a while; however, it took a while for things to settle down, but it was not long before another scandal became the gossip of the regiment.

In addition to our Denmark ventures, we had engagements in France, Belgium and Germany, with concerts at Spa's, schutzenfest celebrations, and freedom marches, plus regimental parades, beating retreat, and Officer Mess nights.

There was a very good system of musical training, which basically consisted of three levels, A3, A2, A1, each level representing advancement in music, and a pay increase. Testing for this was always held with a bandmaster from another band being called in to pass or fail the soldiers. Standards were high, requiring musicians to be able to play set pieces, studies, scales, arpeggios, a theory of music test and in the A1 test, knowledge of arranging and conducting. Band practices were held daily, with work for concert tours, individual and group practice, marching band drill for parades.

The band was hired to play at several concerts and some marching displays for a flower festival in Fourmies, France, and some 230 kilometers from Paris. This was an annual festival, where the town went berserk throwing flowers at one another after having stuffed themselves with food and consumed several vats of wine. Our stay was for four days and our accommodation was two large dormitories complete with beds and washrooms at a holiday camp. Drinking alcohol was a way of life in the British Army and more in particular with military bands who were entertaining the crowds at concerts. In fact, in Fourmies we were given wine at breakfast, the water could not be drunk, especially in France. After our first concert in the town square for the flower festival, we escaped by bus to our holiday camp retreat, where we could relax and of course, drink a few beers after supper. Later in the evening we decided to borrow a couple of boats moored at the lake, row out to the centre and skinny dip. It was past midnight and we were enjoying our swim, when we heard voices shouting from the shoreline. It was our bandmaster with the camp owner shouting and waving for us to come ashore. As we got back on land we were told there could be no swimming after 23:00. A filter across the lake was used after that time; the filter consisted of a series of sharp knives. We must have swum across the filter; still, we were very lucky not to have had some nasty injuries.

The following day the band gave two concerts that were well received and marched in a parade through town, as people lined the streets, throwing flowers and candy. Our evening was free from 19:00 and, tired from the previous evening's antics, I went to bed to catch up on my sleep. I was woken by the bandmaster, who told me that there was a party and I was needed as a piano player. I quickly dressed and got into a waiting limousine, which stopped twice to pick up more passengers, all of them were young ladies. My boss glanced around the car and whispered in my ear, "Ladies of the night, I fear."

On arrival at a big mansion I was taken to where the piano was stored; it was so badly out of tune, I could not play a single melody on it. A young girl said to me, "This is your lucky night, stay and enjoy the fun." My boss and I decided to stay for one drink, socialize for a short while and then leave. There was a large group of important people, local magistrates, a police chief, a prison governor, politicians and doctors, and of course the ladies of the night, forming a large circle and exchanging keys. This was a key party with couples pairing off, dancing to some recorded music, and some finally disappearing into rooms upstairs. My boss finished his drink and then grabbed my arm: "Time for us to go," he said and found the chauffeur to take us back to our hotel. *What a lucky escape!* The following evening, these very same people were making speeches about, citizenship, loyalty, honesty and integrity. *What a sham!* My bandmaster said to me, "Don't look so surprized, the higher the rank, the more decadent the behaviour." How true this statement was, finding this to be true throughout my life, and something I have never forgotten.

Our tour was successful, being asked to return the following year, we returned to Osnabruck tired, but in good spirits after four days of performing.

Our bus journeys were always enjoyable, with the band taking turns in telling jokes and singing the famous rugby songs, our bandmaster would pretend to be sleeping in the front seat, ignoring us but smiling all the while. Of course, there was the usual endless limericks, which always started things off, clean and funny to begin with, and gradually deteriorating to the lewdest of them all:

There was a young lady of Wantage
Of whom the Town Clerk took advantage,
Said the Borough Surveyor; indeed you must
pay her, you've totally altered her frontage!

One of the favourite ones that have always stayed in my mind was 'Rule Britannia'.

Rule Britannia, marmalade and jam,
Three Chinese crackers up your rear end,
Bang, bang. Bang.
Rule Britannia, marmalade and jam,
Five Chinese crackers up your rear end,
Bang, bang, bang, bang, bang.
Rule Britannia, marmalade and jam,
Ten thousand Chinese crackers up your rear end,
BOOOOOOOOOOM!

This was sung with great gusto and was a favourite for the entire band, and would be followed with the invitation for someone else to introduce another limerick by singing: "That was a very good song, sing us another one, just like the other one, sing us another one, do, over to you," after which another song would be sung. The rugby songs were always a hit, but the band would excel in the rendering of "On Ikla Moor Ba tat" with a bandsman reciting the many verses between the chorus, and the 'Whiffenpoof song', breaking into a four-part harmony. Eventually, our repertoire exhausted, the bus would become silent, spare the sound of the engine, and some snoring. On returning to camp we would be given a free day, spending time with our families, followed by rehearsals for our next engagement.

Next on our calendar, was Mons, in Belgium, where we were to play for the celebration of the Second World War Freedom marches. We performed at four small towns in the same vicinity; however, what had not been taken into consideration was the wonderful hospitality, showered upon us by every small town. The band marched through the first town, arriving at the town hall, where there was a champagne reception. Some twenty minutes passed, and it was time to board the bus to the next village, but trying to get the band organized was going to be difficult, and in fact, hopeless! The band were scattered throughout the town hall, chatting to veterans, and having their glasses refilled. I could see our baritone saxophone player; he was swaying from side to side while chatting up an attractive girl, and holding two glasses of champagne. He was wearing a garland of flowers round his neck, and looking at me with a silly grin. I could see that we had a problem. Sat on the steps to the town hall were three more bandsmen, laughing and joking, and being offered more champagne. But it was too late to stop the flow of alcohol, which was homemade, and lethal. Our bandmaster made a wise decision to postpone the remaining marches until the following day, and asked the organizers not to serve alcohol. However, this was ignored, but our senior ranks kept a watchful eye on things, and we managed to complete our tour without further problems.

It seems that my entire military career involved alcohol, the truth being that this was the case throughout the British Army, which resulted in the downfall of many. The difficult thing to learn was when to say *no*, and it took me a long time to master this fine art; in fact, about seventy years. In my defence I might add that all of our engagements involved alcohol, plus the hospitality of our German hosts, and it would seem rude if we had refused a drink. For the most part the entire band followed the rules and would only drink after the performance. Nevertheless, on some engagements, I remember our hosts climbing on the bus with trays of snaps for the band to consume before they played, only to be forcibly removed. They were told to try again, after the band had played.

Dance Band – Myself /Piano, Davy / Bass, Jim / A/
Sax, Thatcher / T/Sax, Don / Tpt, Doug / Drums.

I played piano in the dance band, which consisted of a trumpet, alto and tenor sax, drums, piano and string bass. I rehearsed most afternoons, and some evenings. I can remember receiving the score for Coronation Street, and remarking that it was an awful piece, which would not be around long, yet fifty years later, it is still with us.

We got regular work and extra pay of course, although the public fund and bandmaster took their cuts of 7.5 and 10 percent. Sometimes we were asked to play for extra time, which was always cash for the band—and no cuts. At one time we all bought 'Beetle' wigs to cover our short hair, and were mobbed after one concert in Heidelberg, with girls wanting us to sign autographs on their arms, as they really thought we were the Queen's personal band from the palace. We later received a letter from Buckingham Palace, thanking us for wonderful representation of her Majesty!

The Band was hired to play at the Mons Band Festival, and was billeted at Major Sabre Barracks, sleeping on the top floor. Our first evening meal was a meat dish, which tasted different and a little sweet; it turned out to be horsemeat! Everyone went out to explore the town and find a good watering hole, and meet the other bands in the Festival. There were eight bands performing that year, each presenting a marching display before an enthusiastic crowd. It seemed as though all the bands were in one pub, enjoying the local selection of beers and getting to know each other, despite the language barrier. My partner in crime, Jim Dott, spotted a local guy in the corner, sporting a beret covered with badges and trophies.

Corporal Dott had already decided that the beret was ours for the taking. His plan was to position me at the entrance, whilst he would snatch the beret, and throw it to me. This part of the plan worked well; however, with the beret in my hands, I could see four musicians making their way towards me to retrieve the beret. Thinking quickly, I raced outside the pub, saw a post box across the street, posted it and hid. I was safe, and was not seen. Back at the barracks, I told Jim what I had done. "Excellent plan," he said.

I got up early the next morning and waited for the early post collection, explaining to the postman that I had posted the beret for safety; he just shook his head and handed it to me. The beret was put on display in our band room amongst other acquired treasures from other engagements.

Looking out of the window from the top floor, I could see some activity in the street below; people were going into a bakery and waving to others to join them. Two people saw me and were waving for me to join them, and after a quick discussion, Jim and I got dressed in our blues uniform and went to investigate. At the shop entrance was a priest, who explained that everyone was welcome to come to the Christening breakfast, and we were invited inside and sat down to a huge meal complete with wine. After the meal someone stood up, raised his glass, looked in our direction and said, "God Save the King." I felt I should reply and said, "Vive la France!" The priest roared, "Vive la Belgique," immediately correcting me, but everyone cheered and forgave me. We stayed and enjoyed the hospitality, sitting by the front window looking up at the top floor of the barracks, we saw our bandmaster beckoning to us to join the band.

My life as a Corporal in the band was varied and interesting. My boss was grooming me to be a bandmaster in the future. I played bassoon in the concert band, bass drum, cymbals or baritone saxophone in the marching band and piano for the dance band. I was also given time to try my conducting with the band who seemed to like my style. I spent some time working on harmony and arranging simple hymns for church band, and was soon to be promoted to 'Acting Sergeant', giving me more responsibility.

Entering the sergeant's mess as a young twenty-five-year old fusilier was a rewarding experience. There were some wild characters in the mess, who were always up to pranks on unsuspecting visitors, including firing a Wombat (Anti-Aircraft Gun), in part of a sketch about evacuation from barracks. The entire prank went horribly wrong, after placing a blank round in the breech, firing, followed by an ear piercing roar, which not only made everyone deaf for the next hour, but broke most of the windows in the building.

Each year all the bands stationed in West Germany would assemble in Berlin for the famous Berlin Tattoo, making a vast marching band of over five hundred musicians billeted in an old German Army camp in Spandau. The theme for the pageant was a battle between the Scots and the English facing one another at each end of the stadium, the Scots defending their castle in the morning fog when suddenly the English are sighted advancing towards them as the general alarm is played.

The English bands played 'Army of the Nile', with added riflemen shots on the second beat of the second bar marching towards a Scots Band of Bagpipers, countermarching at the very last moment. This gave the effect of fighting, much to the roar of appreciation from the capacity audience. There was an extravagant finale with massed bands playing National Anthems complete with a visual picture of a crown as some musicians stood with their right arm outstretched holding a small bulb attached to a battery in the pocket. As the floodlights swept through the ranks to the sound of music and musicians peeing, giving an unusual steam effect and adding to the choreography, the crowd rose to their feet asking for more.

I was to sit the entrance exam to enter the Royal Military School of Music as a student bandmaster the following month. I passed and made preparations to move to Knellerhall in Whitton, Twickenham UK. Moving back to England would mean more separation from my wife and children, who would have to stay with family until I had got through the probationary six months. I would then have to look for a place to rent.

CHAPTER 19

STUDENT DAYS – KNELLERHALL 1966–1969

This period of my life was both joyous and sad. I was to achieve my ambition during the next three years whilst at the same time become separated from my wife and family. Trying to relate to the course of events that resulted in our separation was both painful and confusing; there were many factors to be considered, and not wishing to bad mouth my first wife, it was perhaps for the best as we had little in common. Some forty-five years have elapsed since my divorce. Since then, time has been a great healer and having met Rosemary, my present wife, she has been very supportive of me and the children. I only hope our children can forgive us for how we behaved, for they deserve better than what we gave them.

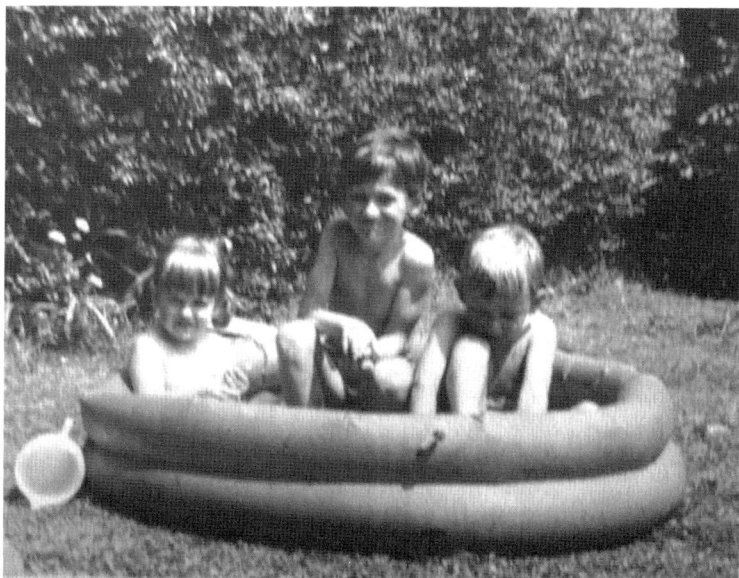

Julia, Clive and Malcolm at Twickenham

Last day before Clive and Malcolm leave for Canada

Arriving at Knellerhall I soon realised that I was a small fish in a very large pond. Our class was known as the Basil Browne class of 66 and consisted of students from Sierra Leone, Mauritius, Nigeria, Sarawak, Australia and sixteen other British Army regiments. We were named as WOC 11 (War Office Class 11) probationary students for a period of six months, after which time we would be told if we were accepted. At my audition I played a part of a Mozart bassoon concerto, a Corelli sonata for violin and an impressive Chopin waltz after which Colonel Browne asked me to stay and sight read some piano accompaniments for other candidates. My audition went well, and I met up with other students and introduced myself. I first met Rodger Tomlinson from the Royal Signals that day and we became good friends (although we later lost that relationship). There were twenty-one new students in WOC 11 including—for the very first time a woman—Zara Bowness from the WRAC (Women's Royal Army Corps). Students were assigned to a company and would work with more senior students who were in their second or third year of study. We were treated with little respect and were constantly teased, belittled and reminded that we were on probation, serving our masters as WOC 11 students.

Our first few days consisted of information meetings, introductions to the teaching faculty, which consisted of two professors; Lieutenant Colonel (Retired) D.A. Pope, OBE. FRCM. psm (Professor of Instrumentation) and Dr. N. Richardson MBE, D.Mus. LRAM. ARCM. LGSM. FTCL (Professor of Harmony and Aural). We were taught daily by both these men and we could not have had better instruction. They were a pleasure to work for, while always encouraging us to do better to improve our musicianship. The school administration, (Lieutenant Colonel B.H. Browne, OBE, ARCM, psm, RE), Director of Music. Colonel C.A. Morris CBE. Commandant. Major F.A.D. Betts (Adjutant). Mr. D. N. Taylor ARCM. LTCL (School Bandmaster). R.S.M. D. Wilkinson (Coldstream Guards).

The class ahead of us was referred to as WOC 1 (War Office Class 1). The task ahead of us was to survive for the next six months and be able to pass the test as a probationary student. We were billeted in rooms above the main building, which became our private domain for some time, where we slept, and spent many hours cramming our homework each night. Our first few weeks were busy with getting to know the schedule and being in the correct place at the right time. After the morning parade we would attend classes in instrumentation, harmony and aural, and in addition to this, there would be company band practice, professors' lessons on secondary instruments, and individual practice. Immediately after supper, there would be three hours of homework, and by 21:00, most of us would congregate in the students' mess for a few drinks, retiring for the night by midnight ready to face another day. During the week there would be full band practice involving students and pupils during which one student would be selected to conduct a piece for a public concert on the Wednesday evening. We waited our turn with fear, hoping we would have some time to study the score beforehand; this was not always the case.

My first piece to conduct was a 'Gypsy Impression' (Black Eyes), which was easy for me; however, later at a full band practice, I was given a difficult work for both band and conductor entitled 'The Wreckers' by Emily Smythe. This was a descriptive, fiery work about the pirates on the west coast of England. Fortunately, I was familiar with this work, and to everyone's surprise, I put the band through their paces, and with confidence. It was at this moment that I realized that I could conduct, and never looked back after this incident. The first homework was completed and returned with favourable comments, both for instrumentation and harmony. I was blessed with perfect pitch and had no problem with aural, scoring one hundred percent. Mike Butcher was from the Australian Air force, and he became close friends with me and Rodger. We were approaching the end of the probationary period. I introduced Rodger to my wife and family in Brighton on a free weekend. On returning to K.H. we were told that our fate had been decided and that we had been accepted as students and could now start to look for a place for our families, later qualifying for a married quarter.

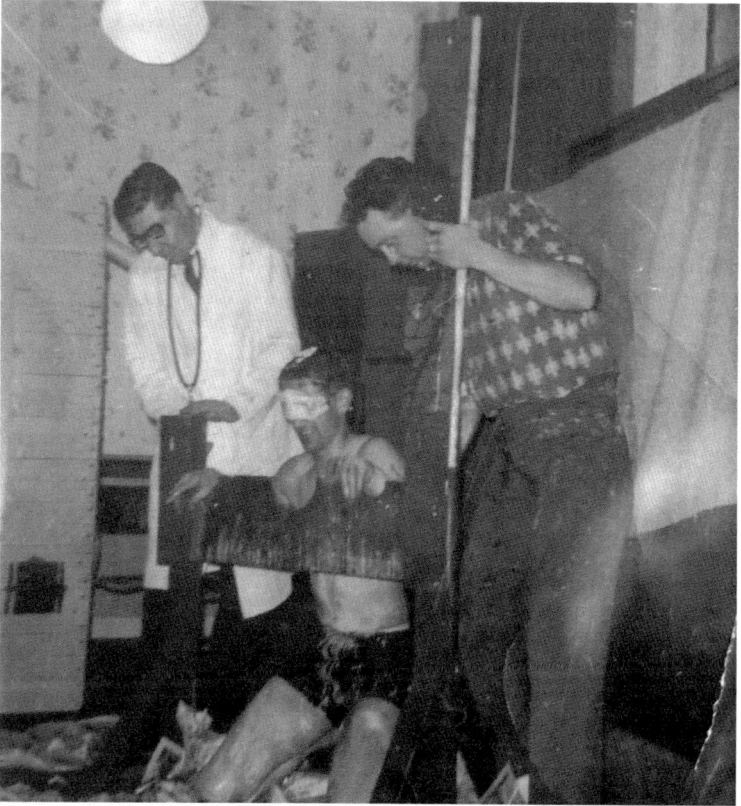

Initiation ceremony, assisted by WO1 students, Charlie and Pete

Each class went through an initiation ceremony conducted in public view by the senior class WOC 1, who came up with a different theme to entertain the audience. The pupils had been dismissed and we were waiting for the next intake, which was the perfect time to have the initiation. We were stripped to the waist (Zara was allowed more appropriate attire) and then locked in a room. We were roped together to the front of a large garden cart, in which the esteemed senior class was assembled. We then pulled the assembly down to the mess in true slave fashion but remained in good spirits knowing that soon, the initiation would mean acceptance as a student bandmaster at Kneller Hall.

I was blindfolded and taken to a room. I remember sitting on bedsprings, and then being lifted into a swing and pushed, my face meeting with a lamb's heart. I had eggs cracked on my head, and I had to suffer an ordeal of fire and water, before finally being led to the stocks. "Tell us a joke!" they yelled. I tried but they responded: "Too clean, come on spice it up a bit!" they yelled as I was pelted with rotten tomatoes. I tried again. "Filthy!" they yelled, as more rotten fruit was hurled at me, with the audience laughing and cheering. Finally, I had to sing 'Rule Britannia', which was found acceptable and I was released from the stocks and invited to drink from the 'yardstick of ale', which contained anything but ale. I was advised to let it spill down my chest, and was then welcomed into the Knellerhall Club, which was only for bandmasters. I have kept my certificate of Initiation, which reads:

"Whereas by virtue of the powers & authority vested in us by the 1966 class, we, the members of the 1967 class welcome student Bandmaster M.C. Scholfield into this ancient and honourable establishment. The aforementioned student passed the ordeal by fire and water and great cacophonous sounds with flying colours and a beaming countenance, given under our seal this 23rd day of September 1966."

We left to change, returned and were officially welcomed, and congratulated as we began our course of studies over the next three years. If we were successful on passing the bandmaster's exam, we would be given a BA (Honours) degree from Kingston University.

The following year, it was our turn to initiate the new students, choosing something different for the occasion, trying to be original with our ideas. Our group decided to have the stage set as a church, going through a mock funeral service, placing each new student in a coffin. Slightly on the irreverent side, managing to get through the ceremony without any serious complaints as the evening concluded with partying and congratulating the new students on being accepted to Knellerhall. After an evening of celebrating, someone suggested that we return the coffin to the funeral home in the high street. We formed a small marching band and proceeded to slow march with the coffin along Whitton High Street. A police car, travelling in the opposite direction, screeched to a halt, made a U-turn, pulling alongside. The policemen asked if we had a body in the coffin, and we were made to unscrew the lid to reveal an empty casket. Everyone was laughing, including the two policemen after we had explained the ceremony; however, we were told that the incident had to be reported and it was in the local paper the following week.

CHAPTER 20

'JIGGS'

Our new Director of Music was Colonel Jaeger, who succeeded
Basil Browne in 1968 at the School. 'Jiggs' as he was nicknamed, had been Director of Music of the Irish Guards where
he had gained a reputation for his outstanding musicianship.
'Jiggs' and other Guard Directors would meet at the Army and
Navy Club in Westminster for lunch during the week, prior to
being appointed Director of Music at Knellerhall. At one of
these lunches my father sat with Colonel Jaeger, and in conversation, mentioned that I was a student at the school in my
third year. When 'Jiggs' arrived at K.H. he was formally introduced to the students and pupils who were assembled on the
bandstand for full band practice. His first announcement was,
"Is there a student Scholfield here today? If so, stand up." As I
got to my feet he added, "Your father sends his regards," and

then made a courtesy. He was known for his whacky behaviour, but I now knew that I had a friend at the top.

After conducting at a concert, I was summoned to go to his office for a conducting lesson, which consisted of vacuuming the carpet, followed by a lesson of how to conduct 'God Save the Queen'. Over the next few months I got to know him well, respecting his talent and knowledge, but having to go along with some of his wild behaviour. He introduced me to an American composer, and I was asked to tell him what scale he was playing, as he fingered an imaginary violin. Watching his fingers move through tones, semitones, open strings and the position of his bowing arm, I could give the correct answer. Despite his happy exterior, 'Jiggs' seemed to be a lonely man, and with few people to share his brilliance with, he would befriend several students—including myself—taking us to swanky restaurants in London. One Christmas Eve he persuaded us to join him, as he would be on his knees, playing the piccolo trumpet. On one of these adventures we drove up to Buckingham Palace at one in the morning, with 'Jiggs' stood on the roof of the car playing *Happy Birthday* for the Queen, then telling a policeman that he knew the Queen personally as we managed to get him to stop before he was arrested. Talented, passionate, outrageous, generous with everyone, a non-conformist would be the best description of him, but a thorn in the side of authoritative ranks above him; he never stood on ceremony, always doing things his way.

In June 1969, in a typically high profile engagement, he conducted the Knellerhall Trumpeters high up on one of the towers at Caernarfon Castle at the Investiture of the Prince of Wales, returning to the mess and keeping the bar open to a late hour. He told his students that if he invited them to join him for a drink and his order was a gin and tonic, then this would mean the student was in trouble. He was not a well man having had several mild heart problems, and was finally hospitalized for a much needed rest. I went to visit him finding him studying the racing form, listening to the latest results from the track, he smiled, and then thrust a five-pound note in my hand saying: "Put this on Two Blues, running in the two o'clock at Kempton Park." Later he was discharged and conducted the massed bands at Windsor Castle for a festival. This was to be his last performance, dying the following day at his home. His dying words—as he replied to someone who said, *Quickly, get Dr. Greene*—were: "I don't need Dr. Greene, he's a gynaecologist. I'm not having a baby, I'm having a heart attack!" At his funeral in the Guard's Chapel at the Tower of London, many came to pay their last respects, with a eulogy given by the Chaplin General of the British Army, who had been a Padre when 'Jiggs' was first promoted as Director of the Irish Guards as a Captain. The Chaplin recalled the first church service with 'Jiggs' conducting his (Avant guard) arrangements of the hymns, after which 'Jiggs' made a comment to the congregation: "I've just had a telegram from God which said 'Watch It'!" There were stories of unpaid gambling debts, restaurant bills from treating numerous people to lavish feasts, yet little provision made for his wife and son. I am told that the Masons, of whom 'Jiggs' was one, cleared his debts, bought a bungalow for his widow and helped with education expenses for his son. I feel extremely privileged to have worked with Colonel Jaeger, probably the most brilliant, influential man to be involved with military music. *Thanks for sharing your gifts with me.*

CHAPTER 21

APPOINTMENT AS BANDMASTER

Having been promoted to bandmaster, I arrived at Templehof Airport, Berlin. Now, I had to get used to the expectations of a bandmaster, holding the rank of WO1 (Warrant Officer Class 1). Ranks below me addressed me as 'sir', and those above me, called me 'Mr. Scholfield'. Reporting to Belfast barracks, Berlin, I was introduced to the band, but could not meet my colonel until later that week. I was replacing Bandmaster Carson, who gave me some good advice with regard to who I could trust in the regiment, selling me his mess kit at a low price. My Band Sergeant was Harry Mann; he was very well respected and a perfect gentleman, and he guided me through my first few weeks. I was twenty-nine years old—younger than most of the musicians—and I was welcomed with a party, where I met the entire band.

Bandmaster Carson departed, and I officially took the reins, with my first duty conducting a church band. I received a message that the RSM, Gordon Chillcott, would like to meet me. But, after arriving at his office, I was ignored as he continued writing at his desk. I left and returned to my office, however, the phone rang, and I was asked to return. I responded to the corporal, "Inform the RSM, if he wants to see me, ask him to come to my office." He arrived shortly after, and I returned the compliment by ignoring him, keeping my head down while writing at my desk. When I looked up, we both laughed. He said, "I can see that we are really going to get along. Come on let's go for a pint at the mess." Gordon became a very good friend, who helped me through a difficult period of my life, giving me advice and encouragement when I was low and needed cheering up.

I was to meet the colonel the following Monday, but was taken out to the New World, which was a Schutzenfest club, with three levels. At ground level, there was a huge assortment of food and beer, and above was a drinking lounge with several bars, including a dance floor. The top floor was reserved for clients who wanted to buy beer by the barrel, which was brought to your table, placed in a cradle, and opened for your consumption by a waiter, who tapped the barrel. At the end of the room was a slide, and for 10pfgs, you could slide down to the dance floor, where there were groups of willing girls to dance with. There was a revolving stage, which presented a different band every twenty minutes, giving lots of variety for the dancers, the like of which I had never seen before. I tried the slide, swooped down into the arms of a blonde, who danced with me for a while and then dragged me up to the top floor, where she lay under a barrel and told me to turn the tap on. Making a hasty exit, I managed to dump her very quickly. There were four of us in our group, staying for the next three hours, ordering bratwurst and drinking our draught beer. We left a few pints in the barrel, and ordered a taxi back to barracks, not like others who had passed out, lying by the entrance in order to sober up.

The following week I met my commanding officer, Colonel Streather, one of the Everest team. He was a keen equestrian, and a bit of a hangover from an anachronistic age. I don't think he liked me from the start, however, the Back Badge parade was next on the agenda, and he was anxious that things would go well and wanted to discuss the music. This was to be an important day as the parade was mounted for all officers, riding horses on loan from the Berlin Police, with the Duchess of Gloucester as the inspecting officer, and colonel of the regiment. Few of the officers had any experience with riding horses; in particular the second in command, who had a few carrots up his sleeve, which he fed to the horse. He would bribe the animal to behave as he approached the saluting dais, where he would hand over the parade. Except for the dress rehearsal when the horse got scared by the sound of bugles, everything went well.

My first officers' mess night with the band playing was the following week, and I was informed that I should include 'Climb every Mountain', especially for the colonel who traditionally had his tune played each mess night. I discovered later that he was tone deaf, and junior officers would request other music in its place: 'The Teddy Bears Picnic', or 'Midnight in Moscow' was chosen some nights, but the colonel would always come and say: "Thank you for playing my tune." If only he knew what was going on, or someone was to tell him, I could have been in trouble, but thankfully it was the best-kept secret in the mess.

As the new bandmaster, I was introduced to the entire mess and was asked to play the bassoon solo 'Lucy Long'. This is the story of a young girl, Lucy, who goes to a dance, has too much to drink, staggers, sobers up, and runs all the way home, and is musically presented in four variations. However, between each one I was handed a gin and tonic to down, as they counted, each drink proved stronger than the previous one. My Band Sergeant was conducting while holding a big grin on his face, and the junior officers were shouting encouragement, cheering as I finished each glass. Still, I passed the test.

1 Glosters concert in Berlin

Europa Day in Berlin 1969

I had my own suite, nicely furnished, in view of Spandau prison from my window, and within walking distance to the Sgts Mess. The RSM and myself were granted the services of a batman who cleaned our uniforms and took care of our needs.

There were some memorable nights in the sergeants' mess, which had an old black Bechstein grand piano sat in the corner of the room. I could not resist the temptation so I began to play, with sing-a-long sessions, and—after the ladies had left—the rugby songs. A popular song in the Glosters was, 'Where be that Blackbird be', an appropriate choice for a West Country Regiment, and with good audience participation. I have included the chorus and verses for you:.

THE BLACKBIRD

(Chorus) Where be that Blackbird to? I know where he be.
He be up yon Sycamore tree, And I be after he!
Now I sees he, And he sees I,
Buggered if I don't get 'en
With a bloody gurt stick I'll knock 'im down
Blackbird I'll 'ave he!
La la la la la la
La la la la la
'Ow's E Father?
(Audience answer) All right!

All me life I'm on the farm, workin' for me keep
Tendin' pigs and chickens, and they cows and sheep

But everywhere I'm workin' one who always mocks me
He hidin' somewhere in the trees, blackbird I'll 'ave he!

(Chorus)

Underneath the open sky in spring we loves to dine
We likes to 'ear the flappin' of the missus washin' line
We listens to a tuneful song, a blackbird or a tit.
But on me vest and underpants he scored a direct hit.

(Chorus)

If I goes out poachin', a creepin' through the fields,
With me old retriever, a followin' at me heels.
If I aim me shotgun at a pheasant in the hay
That bloody blackbird starts his row
and frightens him away!

(Chorus)

No longer can I sleep at night, get peace of any kind,
That bird'll be the death of me, he's prayin' on me mind!
If I chase him long enough, I'll get 'en by and by,
And celebrate me vict'ry with a girt big blackbird pie!

(Chorus)

This song would always be sung last, followed by closing
the bar and going home to bed.

CHAPTER 22

LIFE IN BERLIN

There were two other regiments stationed in Berlin: The Argyle and Southern Highlanders, and the Stafford Regiment, with Roger Tomlinson and Richard Woollcott as directors. Roger had been in my class, and Richard was two years ahead of me. Both Roger and Richard had failing marriages, so I was in good company. Richard was in the barracks across from my office, and came to greet me on my first day at work, inviting me out for an evening at the famous Red Rose Club, with international cabaret. He had won two tickets, which included a free bottle of champagne at a raffle the previous month, and thought I would appreciate a night out with no expense. We arrived at the club, watched some bizarre cabaret, including a man lifting a grand piano, drank our champagne and were invited to join a group of American tourists who took us with them to several other dens of iniquity.

I settled down quite quickly, with lots of projects to occupy me, working late into the evenings, trying not to think about my family, and only wished they were with me.

The Back Badge Parade was a huge success, and my colonel seemed to think more highly of me, congratulating me on my performance with the band. I began to change a few things with regard to the running of the band, putting my stamp on things. My predecessor had been a little aloof, and had a very different approach to things than myself, which was reflected by morale within the band. At my first staff meeting in a Gasthaus near the barracks, I was able to get to grips with some of the problems in the band. By finding out who would support me, I was then able to differentiate between my supporters and the trouble makers.

Not long after my first encounter I had two bandsmen posted, and another two promoted, including Jeff Hinchliffe, who was promoted to Sergeant. Jeff was married to Barbara and had three children, who I got to know over the next year. While having to put up with our returning home late from celebrating after concerts, my wife Rosemary and Barbara became close friends. Jeff confided in me that he had started a career working in a coalmine; on his very first day, he witnessed a man being crushed to death by a runaway cart, resulting in his father endorsing his signing on with the Army. Jeff was later promoted to WO11 as Band Sergeant Major and served the band faithfully for many years after I left. Barbara sadly passed away after a courageous battle with cancer in 2011. I will always remember her as she would scold her daughter Susan, saying: "So help me God, I'll mark you if you don't stop." Susan would thrust out her hand to be punished, followed by her grinning as she offered the other hand for more. Other band members that were supportive were Corporal Sandals, our pianist and clarinet player; Bob Ford, clarinet; Corporal Pearce, percussion; Sergeant Carbin, clarinet; Sergeant Marston, clarinet; Sergeant Bob MacDonald, trumpet, and later, Band Sergeant Major WO11. John Warren, percussion and trumpet, joined us from the Royal Hampshire Regiment at amalgamation. Also there were many more good musicians in the band who were loyal and fun to work with.

I introduced a keep fit run on Friday afternoon, followed by a Happy Hour, and slowly the spirit of the band started to change for the better. Separated from my wife and missing my family made me depressed. I tried not to think about my domestic mess and occupy my thoughts with my new job, occupying my time with planning events for the band.

I was invited to the sergeant's mess as a guest, welcoming me as the new bandmaster to Berlin. I sat next to the RSM, a Welshman, known for his eccentric behaviour of being carried out on parade so as not to get the studs of his boots dirty. There was a small bucket hanging from a hook by my knee, which I was told that I could use in an emergency, if I needed to pee before the toast to the Queen. The evening progressed with wine, passing the port and sherry, and finally partaking of the 'boot', filled with scotch, which I was advised to not swallow, but let the mixture spill down my chest. The evening came to an end with an invitation to conduct the band, followed by a free ride home in a minibus. As I boarded the bus I was joined by three pipers, who I assumed were being taken home, however, later discovering that they were my escort to my room as they played 'Will ye nae come back again' at one o'clock in the morning, marching past the guard room and waking up most of the camp.

At this time in Berlin, the armed forces had separate, distinct areas, namely the British, French and American, each using their own currency within their sector. After a night out visiting various sectors, your wallet would contain not only three different types of money, but also some West German Deutschmarks. Paying the cab driver could sometimes be confusing, although the cab driver always made a good tip. I was invited by some friends to visit the Berlin Schutzenfest in a crowded hall with a large oomph band playing on stage. Waitresses carrying three litre jugs of beer in each hand were serving the tables, not spilling a drop, moving at high speed to serve the thirsty customers. I was invited to conduct the band, after which they formed a circle round my table, which meant that I had to buy them a drink as payment for my conducting. One of my colleagues explained in perfect German, that I was the "Kapellmeister of the Gloucestershire Regiment" and they should feel privileged that I had conducted them; in fact, it should have been them buying me a drink. To my surprise the band withdrew, and I received a free pint; thanking them, I drank it quickly and thought, *What a lucky escape.* We left after a great time of singing all the local Berlin tunes, swaying side to side, with our jugs of beer.

My first concert was at the Zoological Gardens, the Berlin Zoo, with an eggshell stage, and the audience were about 5,000 in number. Needless to say, both we were slightly anxious, as this was my first public concert. There were two other bands performing that evening; a large American Air Force group, and a German TV band, both much bigger than my band of thirty musicians. We were first on the programme and were about to begin, when there was a power outage. I got the band to play 'Hootenanny' from memory. This is a lively piece, which the crowd loved and were dancing in the aisles, people clapping and holding lighters above their heads. The power came back on after five minutes and we began our concert.

Our opening march was 'Entry of the Gladiators' by Julius Fucik, followed by on overture 'Finlandia' by Jean Sibelius. The band played really well, and the audience responded with deafening applause; we continued and played three encores, before we could get off stage. I was bathed in sweat, and found myself actually crying with joy. My boss at K.H. had told me: "This event only happens once in a lifetime, and if, and when, it's time to quit." Fifty years later, I can confirm that he was correct, never having the same experience again. This was my beginning as a new bandmaster, and it felt good to know that I had made my mark.

One of the most unusual places I went to, was the 'Telephone Bar', which was a large hall, filled with tables, and on each table was a telephone with a number. The idea was to look around at the tables, spot someone who you would like to phone, and start dating. It was hilarious! We would phone any table with girls, give them another number from a different table, setting someone up, and then watch the fun, as they would phone back. We could not stop laughing, as we saw the result of our prank. I have often thought that this idea would work here in Canada, and probably be more successful than so-called speed dating.

At this time, the Russians were a realistic threat to the West, causing regiments stationed in Berlin to stage several mass evacuations of families and mobilization of units during their tour of duty. Each exercise was given a code name. There was once when the alarm was raised; I was downtown and therefore knew nothing of the event called 'Operation Rocking Horse'. Realizing that I had been missed, I arrived back at the barracks the following morning.

The RSM advised me that the colonel wanted to see me to discuss the reason for my absence. I remember thinking as I walked towards the colonel's office, *This is unfair; everyone else knew about the alarm, but no one told me!* The RSM was going to march me in to the office—like a Lance Corporal—to which I responded: "You must be joking!" and chose to walk in on my own, asking the adjutant to leave, facing the music, as Colonel Streather confronted me about my absence. I spoke the truth, and just explained I had been away from the camp when the alarm went. But he would not accept this, and awarded me extra duties as Field Officer of the week. I refused to accept his punishment, and responded that if I were going to be treated in this way, then I would resign and so invited my colonel to contact Colonel Jaeger at Kneller Hall, who would support me, and if necessary, replace me with another bandmaster.

Colonel Streather looked puzzled at my response, but made the call to the RMSM in UK. There was a long silence, a brief conversation between the two colonels, followed by the phone being passed to me. "What the hell have you been up to this time? Do you want to stay there, or move to another regiment? The choice is yours."

I decided to stay. My colonel changed his attitude, and forgot about the entire matter, adding: "I guess your guns are bigger than mine." On reflection, I felt like resigning, but not over this incident. It was because of my family situation; I was missing my children, which made me depressed.

One incident that stands out in my mind is 'The Flagpole' charade, where I had been asked by Gordon Chillcott our RSM, to host a fire truck on a Saturday morning, for the purpose of erecting two flagpoles in the barracks, as he was away that day. I agreed, meeting three firemen at the sergeant's mess, where I was having a beer with the paymaster, who insisted that they have a scotch first, to warm them on this cold morning. This was not a good idea, and what followed was a drinking rampage, one scotch after another, ending with both the paymaster and myself, adorned with fire helmets trying to operate a twenty-metre hydraulic ladder. Prior to that the paymaster wanted to drive the fire truck round the square, but thankfully I managed to talk him out of this idea.

The three firemen were drunk and sat laughing. Suddenly there was a loud siren, which indicated hydraulic failure. The siren echoed throughout the camp, much to the delight of some soldiers, who were leaning out of the windows, cheering as they watched the spectacle unfold. The fire truck was thirteenth reserve for the city of Berlin and had been away for four hours to put up two flagpoles, which must have caused some concern back at the fire station. The next thing I saw was a red Volkswagen roaring across the square towards the fire engine. It screeched and came to a halt, and then a fire chief emerged, and started yelling at his firemen. At this point a regimental policeman from our regiment—who had been watching this circus—came over to me and said, "Now might be a good time to leave, sir." Both the paymaster and I made a hasty exit and were the talk of the regiment for the following week. Seeing the paymaster sat in the fire engine, attempting to drive round the square was both alarming and amusing. Thank goodness he did not succeed.

Arriving in Berlin, I attended a mess function where I was introduced to a young lady, Hana Lora. As she was leaving, she shook my hand, leaving a note asking me to meet her at Charlottenburg Station the following day. I went to meet her and we started dating as friends, going to concerts, the zoo, and regular visits for cake and coffee. I gave her a tour of my band set up and took her to the mess for a drink. After a month, I went to take her out for a birthday celebration, travelling to where she lived, on the border with the Communist East.

Her landlady could only tell me that Hana Lora had left suddenly without explanation. Her rent was paid; the apartment empty, and it remained a mystery, until I was summoned to meet with General Bowes-Lyon. As I entered his office, he handed me a file containing pictures of Hana Lora and me going to and leaving various places in Berlin. It seemed innocent enough until I was told that I had been in the company of a spy—counter espionage—spying for the Americans and the Russians. Apparently, I was not to know, and had only given her a tour of the camp. The General said she was probably counting vehicles and personnel strength; however, as a result I would now have to be (green card) cleared by the Americans. I received the clearance the following week and now had a red stamp in my passport, giving me diplomatic status. I would receive a salute at customs. The stamp was removed when I was posted back to the UK.

I received a phone call from Roger Tomlinson, the Bandmaster of the Argyle's, who had a blind date for me. We were to meet two girls downtown in a hotel lobby. I was introduced to an attractive girl, but she could not speak English, which made things a little awkward. I tried my weak German, and she sat and smiled. Meanwhile, Roger was in the back room with her friend; it transpired, that they were sisters. Roger explained later that they wanted both of us to drive through to East Berlin and pick up their brother, dress him in uniform and smuggle him back through Checkpoint Charlie. They were prepared to pay us 1,000 Deutschmarks each! On reflection, it would have been extremely dangerous to be involved with this type of scheme, as sympathetic as we both were.

Later that week, I reported my meeting to the adjutant, who put me in touch with the SIB (Special Investigation Branch), and to my surprise, the SIB already knew that we had been approached. Serving soldiers in Berlin had to be cautious about meeting new friends, and in particularly anyone of a vulnerable nature like me, who was on the rebound from a failed marriage.

During the next few weeks I started getting friendly with a girl called Inga, who worked in a bar. She was very pleasant and I would spend my time with her drinking tea, discussing almost everything from religion to politics, finding that we had a lot in common. She adored classical music, and could name the keys of all the symphonies by *Beethoven*. She was a single mum, and I was hopeful that she was not another spy. However, I was sucked in once more. I became suspicious that Inga was not telling me the truth about her life when she began demanding to see me every day. She was turning up at the barracks at unsocial hours, and expecting to stay the night. I turned her away, so she threatened to send some large male friends round to see me to persuade me to continue the relationship. It transpired that she was pregnant when I met her; the father who was an American Major, had dumped her. I discovered later that she was a high-class call girl, and had set her sights on marrying me. After leaving Berlin she sent me many letters, threatening me that she was coming to the UK to track me down. Some years later I was able to visit Berlin and made contact with her mother, who told me that the American took her back to the States to marry her. It would seem, dear reader, that my two problems in life were drink and women. I made a decision to spend the remainder of the Berlin tour unattached.

I was invited to join the RSM on a reconnaissance mission in a Land Rover with diplomatic plates, which read: 'BRITMIX'. We drove out of the western zone and entered a Russian sector. In the vehicle there was a specialist who was counting tanks and vehicles in the Russian barracks. At one point, we stopped by a house to view the scenery, when a woman rushed out taking pictures of all of us. "I will give these to the Commandant," she shouted. We laughed as the Russians probably have photo identification for all the forces stationed in Berlin.

I took three other servicemen with me to visit East Berlin, changing our money at an American Express Bank at a rate of six East German marks for one West mark. I changed fifty Deutschmarks, which gave me 300 to spend. We went through Checkpoint Charlie, and walked down the main street in East Berlin. Some people stared, others ignored. One man approached me and said, "God *shave* the Queen" not *save*, but we ignored his rude comment. Food and beer was cheap, and chocolate and non-essentials were expensive.

Walking through the town we noticed the cars were from the 1940s and the buses from another century. We found a good pub, had an excellent meal, and drank a few pints, getting into a conversation with some American serviceman, who suggested that we explore the back streets and meet the friendly East German people. On our next visit, we found our way to the back streets and were greeted by a friendly family, who invited us to their house. On the advice of the Americans, we came prepared with packs of cigarettes, which we gave to the family. Cigarettes were a form of currency, and could be used to buy almost anything. The family would be able to buy food, and also a new range for the kitchen. We noticed that everything had a padlock to stop thieves, even the outside washroom. We returned twice more. After our next visit, the family wanted to give us a souvenir from their home, and asked us to pick something from their house. On the wall, was a signed portrait of Adolph Hitler. What a trophy! Unfortunately, on our return through Checkpoint Charlie, the Americans confiscated the portrait. *Imagine the value of that portrait fifty years later!*

On what was to be our last visit to the East, we had decided to visit our local pub. The place was packed with servicemen, Americans, West Germans, East German border guards, Russians, and Brits. Obviously, this was a popular haunt for everyone. Visiting East Berlin meant you had to be dressed in uniform; this was a common rule for any country. Entering the washroom I saw a Russian Major who, looking at my Band crest on my sleeve, said: "So you can sing, can you?"

"Of course I can," I replied.

"Let's find out who is best, Russia or England!" he said. We both arrived back at our tables, discussed our plans and then we stood up, first on deck and sang 'The Wiffenpoof' song in harmony. We received loud applause. The Russians followed with a national tune and were loudly applauded. The Americans soon got the idea and sang 'God Bless America'. We continued with 'Rule Britannia', and so it developed with song after song and of course more beer. The Germans sang their National Anthem, and everyone followed with their National Anthems. There was lots of cheering, hugging and exchanging uniforms, but things were getting pretty lively, and the proprietor, getting nervous, called for the military police to calm things down. It was hilarious. Most of us had mixed uniform at this stage. I had given away my hat and was wearing a Russian cap, almost losing my Sam brown, but managed to hang on to it. Amongst us were all ranks from colonel down to sergeant leaving the pub, arm in arm singing the Saints. The military police arrived and ordered everyone to get back into our correct uniforms. This whole episode made us realize how futile the supposed *Cold War* period was, but it could have had some awkward consequences. After this latest incident my privilege to and from East Germany was withdrawn. I can't think why!

The band were performing at a concert downtown. In the middle of a piece the band warned me that there was a drunk swaying behind me, waving a hundred Deutschmark bill, and yelling "Alta Komaraden". He would not go away. I took the bill and the band played 'Old Comrades' for him as he slumped into a chair in the front row. The following morning, I received a phone call from him apologizing for his behaviour. He invited the entire band to the Schulheis Brewery for a tour; he was the director and owner. I can remember the band returning from this visit. Sitting in the back of two trucks they were merry, while I was playing a piano, which had been given to us at the brewery. I was playing 'Roll out the Barrel' with the band singing at the top of their voices as the truck roared through the barracks.

1 Glosters Band was asked to play as a concert band to celebrate the Queen's Birthday at the Villa Lemme, a seventy-room lakeside complex, which had been the home of the Nazi propaganda minister, Joseph Goebbels, who had used it as a secret 'love nest in which to consummate his countless affairs. Drum Major Bassett and I were summoned by the general in residence at the villa to discuss the Royal visit with Princess Margaret, who would be representing the Queen that day. Our task was straight forward, with the Drum Major providing some waiters, and the band providing the music as the house band. We had no transport to return to our barracks, and were given the number 2 car by General Bowes-Lyons, complete with chauffeur and mini bar in the back seat. Two blocks from the barracks, we managed to persuade the corporal driver to fly the pennant flag, indicating that the general was riding in the car. As we drove through barracks, with soldiers saluting the car, we returned with a V sign gesture from the open back windows, much to the astonishment of all. I received a letter from a secretary at Buckingham Palace, requesting me to submit the music selected for the occasion. It was too tempting not to have a little joke with this, so I included in the programme 'Midnight in Moscow' to which I got a reply stating that this piece would be unsuitable.

The band was well received at the actual function. They played to all the high ranking dignitaries who were milling about with their cocktails, talking out loud and trying to look important. I declined an invitation to a private party with Princess Margaret after the official guests had left, trying to keep away from what would be a drunken soiree. I discovered later that Princess Margaret liked her gin and smoked like a trooper!

There were many memorable nights in the mess, and of course, all of them involved drinking. On one occasion the ORQMS, who weighed over 230 pounds, had fallen asleep in his chair, having consumed a vat of beer. Using a wheelbarrow to ride him home from the mess, we managed to get him to his room and into bed. He was a character from the old school. Each morning he would tap the boiled egg with his spoon, and the German waitress (who could only speak limited English) would take the egg back two or three times until it was to his satisfaction. I placed a china egg in front of him one morning, which he tapped; shaking his head, he looked at me and smiled. After he left the service, I spotted him in the crowd as we were marching through Bristol, and holding a big smile, he gave us the V sign as we marched past.

The band was joined by the band of the Devon and Dorset Regiment to march on a parade held at our barracks. After the parade, I was playing the grand piano in the mess when their bandmaster—who also played piano—joined me. He took the melody and I moved to the bass, playing popular tunes together, we drank, ate and laughed, *until noon the next day*. This was a marathon that I have not done since.

My time in Berlin was coming to a close. It had been a whirlwind, with disastrous affairs, but success with my first band, who were improving musically. My next posting was to be Honiton in Devon, UK. Our new home consisted of a number of rustic buildings, no showers and a poor facility for band rehearsals. Nearest city was Exeter with its famous cathedral, which was over 1,000 years old.

CHAPTER 23
POSTING TO HONITON

I arrived in September 1969, found my new rustic quarters consisting of one room, and went out to explore the town of Honiton which was fairly small and basically a market town originally known for its lace and pottery. I ventured further to the town of Exeter, exploring Exeter Cathedral and the main city centre.

1Glosters was due for a tour of duty in Northern Ireland, with the band included in this trip, although we were classed as non-combatants. The Ministry of Defence had planned for us to be trained medics, enrolling the band on an extensive course at a hospital; we had all passed with honours. Arriving in Londonderry before *Bloody Sunday* our task was to attempt to introduce a Hearts and Minds campaign, giving concerts to various groups. This never happened. We were deployed as a backup guard, manning power stations and other facilities. Our new C.O was Lieutenant Colonel Freeman Wallis, who had been selected to be the colonel for the amalgamated regiments of Hampshire and Gloucestershire. Our new name was to be RRGH (Royal Regiment of Gloucestershire and Hampshire). *What a mouthful.*

I was visiting a community club and was asked, "Are you Protestant or Catholic?"

"Well, actually, a bit of both," I said. On duty one night I decided to score one of the music entries for the Eurovision Song Contest, which was being hosted in Malta that year. I rather liked the Irish entry 'All Kinds of Everything' sung by a local girl from Londonderry. Her name was Rosemary Browne or Dana as she called herself. I spent the evening listening to a tape of this tune, scored it for band and wrote out the parts for the band to play. Listening to the competition, I discovered that it had won! That very next morning my band played this arrangement on parade and by noon I had a phone call from Screen Gems Columbia who wanted to hear my arrangement with a view to purchasing the score. My score was picked up by courier and taken to London where a professional group played it and accepted my work. I was asked how much I wanted for it. Having absolutely no idea I phoned Colonel Jaeger at the RMSM who first congratulated me then informed me that the cost was three shillings and nine pence per measure, plus a copyright fee. I cannot remember how much I actually received but what pleased me more was the fact that I had my own arrangement published. Arriving back from a meeting one day I found my band president, Major Jarman, who fancied himself as a musician, attempting to conduct the band on parade. I took the baton from his hand and suggested respectfully that he leave to meet me in the colonel's office to discuss this behaviour. Later, my colonel supported me and informed Major Jarman that he was out of order.

RSM Chillcott, the paymaster and myself, were driven over the border and found a quiet pub to have a drink. We were all dressed in uniform, which attracted attention as we walked in, but we met some friendly people and shared a few drinks with them. I saw a piano in the corner of the room, so I walked over to it and played a few tunes. My audience enjoyed 'When Irish Eyes are Smiling' and 'Danny Boy', but were not so keen on my six bar rendition of 'God Save the Queen', which I managed before we left in a hurry. The local Irish people were very friendly, yet divided by their religious beliefs and fanatical with regard to politics. In pro-Protestant parts, even the curbs of the pavements were painted red white and blue, and windows showing the Union Jack. The Army held weekly dances for the troops, which were well attended by the local girls. The ratio of young women to men was 7-1, with most males leaving to find work in England. The troops had plenty of choices for a partner to dance with, and many soldiers married Irish girls after their tour of duty in Northern Ireland. At the beginning of our tour, relations between the soldiers and the public were reasonably good, but soon deteriorated towards the end of our time in Londonderry. A young woman who was pushing a pram containing a bomb, was let into the camp. Having left the pram in a barrack room, it exploded, killing two soldiers.

Having several soldiers murdered by the IRA, our tour of duty finally came to an end.. The band had planned to give a public concert in the centre of Londonderry, but it had become too dangerous to for us to perform; things were getting ugly. It was not long after our departure that the incident involving paratroopers using live ammunition in place of the rubber bullets took place. This was in retaliation to the loss of some of their soldiers. The incident became known as *Bloody Sunday*.

Marching through the town to cheering crowds, we arrived in Honiton, and back home to Heathfield Camp.

Mayflower 70 celebrations, held in Plymouth, involved several military bands including the Ghurkhas, The Glosters and The Light Infantry, with Eric Slater as the bandmaster. It was suggested that all bandmasters give each other a forfeit, which meant doing something goofy on stage, and hopefully get away with it. My assignment was a marching display with the Corps of Drums, and my forfeit was to salute the house band as my band marched off parade, instead of the VIP stand. On completion of the forfeit, I then gave my task for the Light Infantry Band, who were to include eight bars of music— 'The STRIPPER'—as they played music for a medieval dance group. There were some strange looks, but the forfeit went well. I was with the Ghurkha bandmaster, Ben Bentley, who enjoyed both pranks, but now wanted to know what he must do. Eric Slater decided that during a Latin piece that the Ghurkha band had to play, everyone in the band would crouch down on the last beat and yell "Oooooo!" I had tears in my eyes as the band performed. I remember later that the three of us drew our swords and slow marched past the main gate, attracting some strange looks from people. The Director of Music who was running the show, must have known about our behaviour, but never said a word.

I became involved with a musical that the Anglican Church was producing. I became the stage manager and performed in one Victorian scene. Both Clive and Malcolm came to live with me, and I was given a married quarter for them to live with me. I now had to be organized, posting menu choices on the kitchen wall, buying canned potatoes, and putting out their school clothes each night, ready for the morning. The organist, Helen Blackmore, offered a place in her private school in Collumpton not far from Honiton, which I accepted. Helen was very helpful giving me some good advice and caring for the boys. She was divorced from the Blackmore family but left the marriage with so much pain she did not want anything from the Blackmore estate. She lived with her mother who had been the lighthouse keeper at Land's End; both were eccentric. Helen started to get closer, but the feeling was not mutual.

Christmas time was approaching and we managed to get through it. Major Morris, the families' officer, invited me and the boys round for Christmas dinner. Shortly after, my wife suddenly appeared on the scene without warning. Things were not going to work out from her point of view. She took the boys and returned to Burgess Hill. Even now—some forty-three years later—I find it painful to write about my feelings, and I hope my boys have forgiven me. I handed back my married quarter and moved back into barracks. My wife informed me that she was filing for a divorce as a petitioner. I would be on the receiving end as a respondent.

There was an amalgamation of our regiment with the Royal Hampshire Regiment approaching. I was working on planning the music for the big day. I had been appointed as the new bandmaster, selected above five other senior directors. New buttons were ordered, hat badges ready and new banners made for the music stands. Also, we had special banners made for our Fanfare team.

The parade was one month away, when suddenly everything was cancelled. There was a General Election, which resulted in the Tories, led by Edward Heath, defeating the Harold Wilson Labour Government. First on the agenda was to restore the identity of each proposed amalgamation; however, the band was to become one, with the Royal Hampshire Band joining us. My band would remain the Glosters Band. It would be over seventy in strength. I was given one year to reduce the size to thirty-five, by offering redundancy to those band members who did not wish to stay, or be given a transfer. This was an upsetting time for some, while others welcomed redundancy, or even the option of a transfer. My own Band Sergeant was not too happy but finally opted for redundancy, which was in his best interest. He was replaced by a younger man by the name of John Warren from the Royal Hampshire Regiment. Bruce Chittock was one of my best musicians and he also applied for redundancy. However, he did not qualify; he expressed a view that he and his wife were from the Mormon Church, and wanted to make this a lifetime commitment. I filled out a form stating that he was a below average musician and would be no loss to the band. He thanked me profusely, and I received an email from him in 2012, thanking me again. He is now a Minister for the Church living in New York with his wife Heather and family.

I had decided to sell off some of the older instruments to raise enough money to buy ten new Bb clarinets, and solve the problem of poor intonation from the woodwind section. My first thought was to use Ken Desmond from Boosey and Hawkes of Regent Street. He was a good friend, and would give me a fair assessment. He arrived, and after a very quick look offered me much less than I wanted, to which I said that I would consider the offer. He then took me out to wine and dine me in true Boosey and Hawkes fashion, involving too much to drink, resulting in Ken needing assistance getting to his bed.

I received a phone call from a friend in Exeter who wanted me to join her at a nightclub. I made a very poor choice of attempting to drive, and I slipped out the back gate, avoiding the guard at the front gate. It was raining and with poor visibility I drove a Riley 1.5, which my Aunt Doffy had given me. I was driving too fast and as I approached the notorious 'Fenny Bridges', I skidded on a corner, hit a mud bank, and the car turned over on its side, somersaulting down the hill. I was terrified. I had totally lost control and jumped into the back seat protecting my head with my hands as the car tumbled down the hill for a good distance, narrowly missing trees and finally coming to a standstill at the bottom of the winding treacherous road.

I heard a voice say, "Hang on, I will pull you out." A truck driver had seen my headlights flashing from side to side and knew that someone was in trouble. It was late evening as I was pulled from the car and made to walk up and down to clear my head. Fortunately, I had no major injuries, except a nasty gash in my leg that would need stitches.

A police car and ambulance arrived at the scene of the accident. The policeman was from Honiton, and recognized me. "'Good evening, sir, what have you been up to this time?" I was breathalysed with a *negative* result. Paddy the policeman added: "Lucky this time, sir. I have written in the accident report, cause of the accident was dog in the causeway!" This was surely a wakeup call to change my reckless style of life, but it would, however, take me a few more years before I changed my drinking habits. I was taken to hospital to get some stitches in my knee and glass removed from my hair, nothing serious. I ordered a taxi back to Heathfield camp and limped back to my bed. My colleague Ken left the next morning and I went to collect the logbook from a garage at Fenny Bridges, which was all that was left. The car was smashed on both sides with the front part of the roof crushed to the steering wheel. If I had not moved to the back during the crash I would have most certainly been crushed. The crash was frightening to realize that I could have killed someone or myself through my reckless behaviour.

I discussed the instrument offer with my Band Sergeant, who suggested getting a second opinion as a result of the low quote from Boosey and Hawkes. He knew of a small music shop in Portsmouth, which he had dealt with previously and had always been more than satisfied. The shop owner arrived with his wife and spent four hours checking my instruments on offer. I was asked what instruments I wanted to buy. My plan was to purchase ten new 929 clarinets and improve the intonation of the band. He suggested that no money would change hands, just the instruments. I could hardly believe what this meant. He was offering me twice the amount that I had been offered by Ken Desmond. *We had a deal!* I took the instruments to his shop later that week, where there were people already waiting to buy my instruments. I picked up the ten clarinets and was invited to the back room, to receive a money gift for bringing him the business. I phoned my Band President who agreed that I could accept this. In the Army, we had to always be careful about this sort of thing.

I had purchased a shotgun and started to go hunting on a farm some ten miles from Honiton, without any success, except accidently killing an owl that had startled me. Weeks later and I was still having nightmares about this incident; hundreds of owls staring at me through my window at night. I would inform the local police on each occasion that I was using my shotgun.

It was at this time that I sank to my lowest ebb, feeling depressed, drinking heavily, and not looking after myself. My appearance became scruffy, arriving late to conduct the band after a late night of drinking. After one binge, I stumbled back to my room, and thinking about suicide, I attempted to load the shotgun. Fortunately, I was too drunk and could not get the gun to work. Sat in my office the following morning, I had a visit from the Medical Officer, who came as a friend to advise me to get some help, telling me that I could not continue like this. I took his advice and made an appointment to see a psychiatrist who, after a lengthy interview, prescribed pills for my depression. What I was going through was a mental breakdown. I was unable to cope, and needed a long rest. I flushed the pills down the toilet, determined to sort myself out.

The Monkton Court Hotel, Devon

CHAPTER 24

MONKTON COURT HOTEL

I was a regular customer at the Monkton Court Hotel, situated just outside Honiton. Originally this hotel had been a Monastery; an artist discovered plans of the original building in 1970, but have since been lost. The hotel had nine bedrooms, a kitchen garden, tennis court, a small golf putting area, and was a three-star AA (Ashley Courtney) recommended listing. Situated on a busy A30 road to Exeter, it has attracted a constant flow of customers, despite the existence of the Honiton bypass. The staff were local people from Monkton, friendly and helpful, serving excellent meals including Monkton duckling, and the famous Devon cream teas. The chef was a white South African who, despite his involvement with the occult, was an experienced cook. It was said that he was a 'white witch' and had predicted the death of a baby for a woman, actually telling her where and when the child would die. He asked me for my keys for a night, telling me the following morning that he saw eight people sat round a table, which would later be my family.

At breakfast one morning, the chambermaid mentioned that room 7 had not yet come down for breakfast. She was told to use her passkey to enter the room, where she found the guest dead in his bed. The police, doctor and coroner were called, who after examining the body, confirmed that it was a death by natural causes; our guest had died in his sleep, but now there was a problem of removing the body. There was only one possible way out, which was down the main stairs, past the front desk and out into the courtyard. We descended the stairs carrying the coffin to the look of astonished American tourists, who were booking in. I remember asking Mrs. Parrott, what would happen with the room, to which she replied: "Open the window, change the sheets, and rent the room again."

The headwaiter was a Spaniard called Manuel, who would charm the patrons with his performance of cooking steak Diane at the table. But unknown to the customers was that he was changing labels on wine bottles to make a bit extra. Manuel would serve a round of three gin and tonics, followed by a subsequent order which would be only one gin poured on to a silver tray; he would share the gin, pour back into the glasses, top up with tonic and serve. The Monkton Court Hotel was so similar to the Hotel in Torquay used for the filming of Fawlty Towers, complete with a Spanish waiter named Manuel, and a dead guest.

My dance band played at the hotel on Friday evenings for dinner and dance functions. I had an official military function to attend and needed a respectable partner to accompany me. All of the females I knew were not that respectable. It was going to be a dress up affair; mess dress for me and my escort in an evening gown. The owner, Charles Parrott, suggested that I take his daughter, Rosemary. She accepted my invitation, and this was the beginning of a good relationship, ending in marriage. Rosemary was divorced and had four children: Amanda, Simon, Sarah and Emma. I was awaiting for my divorce hearing, which I expected would be in the near future. Rosemary and I had a great night and started dating with a view to marriage. My depression vanished as the future now looked a lot brighter. For the divorce hearing, my colonel suggested that I use a method called 'King's Proctor', which meant that all the dirty laundry was sealed in an envelope, handed to the judge, and only used if the case did not go to my advantage. However, the judge—who I believe new my colonel—adjourned the case, wanting to speak with respondent and petitioner in his chambers. I was being granted a decree nisi (forthwith) from the courtroom, which would enable me to get married to Rosemary before the regiment left for Minden in Germany, later that month. I had visitation rights to my family. This was the first decree nisi given in the county of Sussex. Normally, there would be a wait of three years. I proposed to Rosemary, she accepted, and her father threw a large engagement party for us at the hotel. We made hasty wedding plans, booked a registry office for the ceremony and had a wonderful reception at the Monkton Court Hotel. We had a two-day honeymoon before we flew to Minden, West Germany, our next posting.

Wedding reception 1971

Wedding guests

Prior to my divorce and subsequent marriage, I could enjoy the very large band with its big sound, before any of the upcoming changes took place. The band was hired to play for a parade of Veterans, and during the final march past the statue of 'King Billy', it was traditional for the band to play 'Old Comrades'. I decided it was time for change. We played 'St Louis Blues' to liven things up. My new Band Sergeant said, "You are going to be in trouble for this one, sir!" Later I received many compliments, including a telegram from Lord Slim (Burma Star Association): "Well done, at last we get to march to some lively music!"

My fanfare team was now double the size to eight players. We were hired to play one fanfare in Bristol for the International Tupperware Women of the Year. We played fanfare for a dignified occasion by Sir Arthur Bliss. The main entertainment was Acker Bilk, playing 'Stranger on the Shore'. As he stood on centre stage, during the middle eight of the tracks, he walked to the wings and had a shot of scotch, then returned to finish the act. After the performance, he befriended my fanfare team, pushing in front of the entire buffet queue and plying them with drink. I was driving a van and was therefore drinking only ginger ale, and had promised Peggy Parrott— wife to the owner of the Monkton Court Hotel—that I would present my fanfare team to play for her husband's birthday as a surprise. We did attempt this, however, things did not go quite according to plan.

Peggy—the mother of Rosemary—liked me from day one, whereas Charles Parrott took longer to accept me. Still, over the next twenty years, he became a very close friend, and generous father-in-law. I was invited to attend luncheons at the local Rotary Club, and was a frequent guest at the Conservative Club, to which Charles had invited me. Charles was a mason and held the position as Grand Master of the south-west of England. I had been approached several times by colleagues at Kneller Hall, who were masons, but it did not appeal to me at the time; of course, had I realised that this was a sure promise of promotion to join the club, then my response might have been different. The cliché: "It's not what you know but who you know," is so very true, and explained to me later why some rather 'musically untalented' people were promoted over the really gifted musicians. The best example of this can be best understood, when the Director of Music of the Army, stopped a student bandmaster in the middle of a rehearsal and shouted: "What about the big senza rall at the end?" to which we all laughed, especially when the word *senza* means without!

Honiton had a small nightclub called The Pit, which churned out cheap pop music for the masses, but occasionally brought in some live bands. I had a phone call one morning from Monty Sunshine, who had been hired to play at the club, and wanted to borrow some Manhasset stands for his band. He gave me three free tickets for the event, which I accepted and enjoyed his performance that evening, listening to live traditional jazz.

My fanfare team were hired to play on the balcony of a large department store in Exeter at Christmas time. The team assembled, I stood on the opposite side of the street to conduct, when a double decker bus passed through between us, making things a little more exciting. But we did manage to finish together.

Charles and Peggy Parrott were supporters of Dogs for the Blind and sponsored their annual get together at their Monkton Court Hotel. Opposite the hotel was a country walk to the Dumpton Hill Fort, where the dogs and their owners were going to attempt the climb. I was approached to provide music for the event and brought my complete band to perform. All the proceeds from the day went towards the cost of training Dogs for the Blind. The scene was set as dogs with their owners, clambered up the hill with encouragement from onlookers cheering above the sound of the band. It was an excellent day for the event, with a record amount of donations.

Rosemary and I got married on the 15 January 1971, and flew to Minden a week later. My stay in Honiton had been sad at the beginning, but I left with a good feeling that life was going to be happier now.

CHAPTER 25

POSTING TO MINDEN 1971–1973

Before our move to Minden, we had decided to take the children with us for the first year, and then place them in a good Catholic boarding school in England.

We did not get off to a good start. Our luggage had been left in Honiton. For three days we had to survive in the clothes we travelled in, but to console us we were moving to a fully furnished three-bedroom house. Arriving in January with the furnace already lit, we walked into a warm home, organized by my Band Sergeant John Warren. I would need transport getting to and from work to my home, and started looking for a second-hand car. The bandmaster of the Green Howards, Graham Pike, had offered me a second-hand Volkswagen, but first I had to master a German road test before I could drive legally.

Time was short; someone gave me the answers to the test. It was multiple choices, using a, b, c, d, and e. I wrote a tune on manuscript, which got me through the exam. I entitled my music 'I travel the Road'. Feeling slightly guilty, I passed but made sure I studied the German road signs before I attempted to drive. I drove for the first time the next morning, finding it a bit more exciting than the sleepy town of Honiton, and I was now driving on the other side of the road. We settled in our new home and started to learn some German to help us get along better with the local town's people.

1Glosters Band had a busy season ahead of them. I was working at rehearsing music for all the engagements. During Schutzenfest season, we had to be careful not to overbook the band as they needed a break between engagements. One of the major headaches was alcohol, which was available every-where, and at any time. Drinking and driving became a major issue, and the breathalyser was introduced for the first time. I proposed that we build our own bar in a barrack room, make it professional, and with the colonel's blessing we went ahead.

My musicians made a great impression, so much so that my colonel thought that other groups within the regiment could follow our style. One particular engagement at Bad Rothenfelde, some of the band travelled in groups, while the remainder made their way on the bus. One of the cars had the complete tuba section travelling together. They had decided to stop for a few drinks on the way, and misjudged the time for travel. The concert was scheduled to begin at 14:00, with the tuba section finally arriving late at 14:20. We were already seated and awaited their arrival. Of course they needed the bathroom, a request that I denied and made them suffer with red faces and legs crossed until the interval. During the 'Overture Poet and Peasant', by Von Suppe, they all took a breath at the same time during a solo passage. The band almost collapsed with laughter; however, we got through it. The tuba players were fined one share of their pay for their performance, never travelling together for any future engagements.

Most of our engagements were concerts at local towns, performing at health spas, Bad Rothenfelde, Bad Salzluflen, Bad Oyenhausen, all of which had good band performance stages, complete with a sound shell. At one of these spas, we played the Post Horn Gallop. Accompanying our soloist and to make the piece more interesting, Band Sergeant Warren was running from one place to another during the eight bars rest, but tripped and lay sprawling in a flower bed causing the post horn to bend in two.

Our children were not happy at the Forces school in Minden. We had previously arranged for them to attend a boarding school in Sidmouth UK, near the Monkton Court Hotel, which the children could visit at weekends to see their grandparents. Emma was too young and would remain with us. At Easter the children were fitted with their new uniforms and set off for the convent. The Government paid all school fees, as I could not have afforded this expense, which was more than my salary. The Convent of the Assumption was a well-run boarding school, according to the stories from our children, who have happy memories from those years.

Rosemary became pregnant, which was planned; our new arrival would be in March of 1972. Alex was born at midnight on Feb 28 1972, but we decided to make him wait a minute, so he could have a birthday every year on March 1.

The band was tired and I was exhausted from a week of demanding concerts. We were not producing anything of worth, so I stopped the band and gave them the day off. We got changed into civvies, opened the bar and relaxed. Ten minutes later, I received a phone call to say that we were getting a visit from a general in the next fifteen minutes. There seemed little point in trying to cover up what we were doing. The general walked in followed by my colonel, adjutant and RSM. The look on their faces was priceless. I stood to attention and said, "Good morning, sir, what's your poison?"

The General replied, "A small brandy would be fine." Everyone relaxed, and then he asked me: "Do you do this often?"

"Oh yes," I said. "Every Monday," which was followed by lots of laughter. There was a look of relief on the face of my colonel, who told me later that he was pleased that I had not tried to hide what we were doing, adding that "honesty (in most cases) is the best policy".

That summer, I received a call from my ex-wife, saying that she could not cope any longer with the boys. Roger Tomlinson had moved in with her and was stationed in Northern Ireland. The boys told me later that they did not get on with him as a step-father, and they had decided to run away and join me in Germany. Fortunately, the boys were found before they got very far, hiding in a field reading the *Beano*. Clive was eleven and Malcolm nine years old, and they had blankets, cans of beans, a gas stove, eggs, but alas, no money. After the incident, they were told that they were coming to Minden for a visit; in fact, it would be a permanent move. I had to apply for a bigger quarter to accommodate everyone in preparation for the school holidays. I spoke with the families' officer, who arranged for my family to live in two quarters (made into one). It was two miles from the camp, in the town of Buckeberg. My family was now eight in number, while my daughter Julia, stayed with her mother. We now had a combination of *hers, mine and ours*. The Scholfield bunch!

There was some adjusting to do, if we were going to survive as a family. Clive and Malcolm joined Amanda, Simon, Sarah and Emma at the convent. Later the children told us stories of what went on when they travelled together from boarding school. They had fun on the train; getting into a carriage compartment and wanting it for themselves, they had put up a notice that read: 'Measles'. This kept other passengers out.

Living at the convent was again, quite unique. It was a school for boys and girls, whose parents worked for the Government, or who travelled frequently and were unable to give their children a stable education. Run by Catholic nuns—and some outside help in specialist areas—the school was situated less than half a mile from the sea. The Convent of the Assumption was built in 1906, situated in beautiful surroundings in the town of Sidmouth. The food was not that good, however, edible. I am told that Simon had trained the school dog to sit outside the open window and take unwanted morsels of food. Not only had the children had the basis of a fine education, they had endured many adventures, and they often talk about the fun they had during their childhood years. The school is still operating, but now run by the Anglican Church. A book has been published of those years, and I am told my children are mentioned in several places. I would never have guessed!

CHAPTER 26

BAND ENGAGEMENTS

The band played for many schutzenfest celebrations. Of course, these people were the old Hitler youth, although they would never admit it. We provided marching bands, concerts, and dance bands for their festivities, which would spread over several days. The German people certainly know how to party and entertain their guests. The band had been hired to play in a nearby town of Neustadt (New town), outside the Dresdner Bank. Any new business customers were being offered tax breaks on their accounts. We played for one hour, and I went to get the payment for the gigue from the bank manager, who paid me 1,000 Deutschmarks in cash, thanked me and asked if we could do it again. I assumed that he meant another time in the year. "No, right now!" he said. I asked the band who wanted to stay; most said yes, and we played for another hour and a second fee, which I divided evenly between the remaining musicians.

We received a letter of complaint in the local newspaper, spotted by our press officer who could read and speak German. Opposite the band room was an apartment building. Every morning a nurse would return home from duty at 08:00 and try to get some sleep. However, at precisely the same time, the band would begin marching opposite the apartments, playing German drinking songs 'In Munchen steht ein hofbrau haus'. The director of Schulthaus Brewery also read the complaint, and replied to the letter saying that the reason the band did not sound too good, was because they were not drinking enough beer! The following day a beer truck delivered forty cases of beer for the band. The story made the second page of the National Press (Daily Mirror) with the heading: "Band without enough OMPH!" We changed our rehearsal time for the nurse, and received a thank you letter from her.

My parents visited us in Buckeberg, and spent two weeks visiting places of interest. My father could speak German, as he had taken this as a second language in school. In fact, he was really quite fluent. He went to the bank to change some traveller's cheques and had been waiting for the cashier to change to give him his money. There seemed to be a problem, and she had to consult with another colleague. After waiting another ten minutes, my father spoke in German with a loud voice. All heads in the bank turned and were looking in our direction. The money instantly arrived, and there was some smiling and shaking of hands; it seemed that this was an apology. Later.

I asked my father what he said in the bank. "Not much," he said, "just asked why it was taking so long. 'Do you have to get permission from the Fuhrer?'"

After a long concert I was relaxing, having a beer, and I happened to get into a conversation with a man sat near me. He wanted to thank the band for our concert, and in particular, the choice of music on the programme, which included several German pieces: 'Old Comrades', 'The Merry Widow', and some German drinking songs. He told me that he worked as a therapist in a mental home, introducing some different methods to help people. He believed that medication was not the answer for most of the patients, and was working on a project involving acting. He would choose a period of time in history, dressing everyone—himself included—in the costume of that era, which would last an entire week. Having achieved some very impressive results using this unusual therapy, he asked if my band would consider visiting the *home* to give a concert later that month, assuring me that it would be one of the highlights for his group of forty people. The home housed some one hundred people, suffering from a variety of mental issues, including epilepsy and depression. There was an assembly line, beginning with patients placing round pegs into round holes at one end up to a full assembly of car springs for Volkswagen.

We arrived at the home later that month and gave a very successful concert to an appreciative audience, who returned the compliment by treating us to a short musical performance with guitars and drums. Before leaving, I extended an invite for the group to visit our band and spend the day with us.

A few weeks later our guests arrived at the barracks, where we treated them to rides in big trucks, and two games of soccer. They were invited for refreshment to our band bar, enjoying drinking beer; all medication had been stopped the previous day, and they were encouraged to join in the fun and socialize with my band. They sang songs and told jokes; they had great interaction with everyone, and there were two doctors along with several helpers to ensure their safety. We finally managed to get them on their bus, singing and waving as the bus departed. I was told later that on arrival at the home everyone went to bed without problems, falling quickly asleep. There was an eighty percent reduction in epileptic seizures that following week and fewer cases of depression. What these people so desperately wanted was to be treated like the rest of us, and to be able to share with others, not kept in a home with daily medication. Loneliness must be the biggest disease in the world.

Colonel Freeman Wallis was very supportive to the band. His favourite piece of music was 'In the Mood', by Glen Miller. He decided that the band looked scruffy with our ill-fitting uniforms. His plan was to have the entire band measured by a bespoke tailor from the CSSD (Command Service Supply Depot) in Hannover. This professional tailor had made uniforms for Adolph Hitler, so we were told. I asked how much this would cost.

Smiling, my colonel said: "To you, nothing. The officers will take care of payment."

I took my band to Hanover, to be measured for new uniforms, adding a *Blues* dress uniform and mess kit for myself. The band was to be dressed in red tunics, complete with a blue pith helmet with a spike. Two weeks later the uniforms arrived. The band looked sharp, with made to measure tunics and pants.

The following Monday my colonel summoned me to his office, informing me that I was to escort a driver with a three-ton truck, full of single malt scotch, and deliver this to the tailor in Hannover as payment for goods received. On our first parade I was wearing a pith helmet, which I found it did not really suit me. Returning to my office, there was a large ten-inch nail taped to my door under my name, earning me the nickname of 'The Nail'. *The forage cap looks better on me, don't you think?*

1 Glosters Minden

CHAPTER 27

KNELLERHALL INSPECTION

Every band in the British Army was scheduled for a Knellerhall Inspection. This was to see how the bandmaster ran the band, and if he was well respected by the regiment. It was my second year as a bandmaster and still I had not been inspected. Finally, I phoned and asked if I was on the list for that year, and was informed that they were not inspecting my band. There had been good reports of the progress made by the band in the press, and there was no need. However, it was agreed that I would be inspected in the near future.

The following month I was given a date for the inspection. I now had to choose something different and unique for an overture. My Band Sergeant suggested one that the director would not know: 'Der Frosche Koenig' (King of the Frogs). We located the score, tried it and we all liked the piece. It was challenging, yet, it had plenty of colour, contrasting dynamics, and double reed parts for oboe. We spent the next few weeks preparing for the inspection, which would include, marching band, concert band and dance band. There were two groups for the dance band, a small quartet, and a fourteen-piece James Last style group. Marching band was in good shape; we rehearsed on a regular basis with the Corps of Drums.

We arranged a dinner night in the WOs and sergeants' mess, on the request from the inspecting officer, Colonel Bashford, who had risen through the ranks, as all bandmasters had to.

The day arrived; first on the agenda, was the mess dinner. Colonel Bashford met my senior ranks and was able to chat informally with them, so that he could find out what they thought of me. There was a considerable amount of drink consumed, and I recall seeing one of my band sergeants in deep conversation with the colonel; there was no need to worry, everything went smoothly.

The following cold November morning, the Band and Corps of Drums were performing our marching display. Shivering at the side, he whispered to me, "Can't you cut this short? It's bloody cold out here." We cut the last part, and gave the band a break. I offered him a brandy in my office to warm him up. Concert band was next with me conducting the overture, which he really liked and told me he was going to take it back to use at KH library. Sight-reading followed this for the band and myself. He had chosen overture 'Fidelio', by Beethoven. His only opera, which we did not have in our library. He had already gone through our music to see what we had, and brought with him several scores which were not common to most libraries. Slowly, we began the overture and gave a fair performance. He commented: "If you took it much slower, we would still be trying to finish it!" My Band Sergeant was then tested for his conducting. All was well.

At lunch in the mess, he commented that the band was impressive. The afternoon was for the two dance bands and checking the accounts and interviewing some of the band. The day came to an end, I could now relax, and everything could not have been better. The band president called me to his office, where my colonel was sat with Brigadier Brinkley and Colonel Bashford. There were four ratings for a band: below average; average; above average, and outstanding. We had scored an above average. My colonel congratulated me and then stated: "We are going to lose you to another band." Colonel Bashford then told me I had been promoted to Divisional Brigade Bandmaster of the Light Division at the Royal Green Jackets Depot in Winchester, with three weeks to pack my bags and report for duty.

Having worked hard with the band and made so many friends, I was reluctant to leave. The success of the band had been largely due to the influence of John Warren, who was my right hand man. He was an excellent musician and had good administrative skills. I would miss this luxury. I was going to a training school for boys in Winchester, which was a feeder school for the bands in the light infantry. I would be marching at 140 paces to the minute! One of my colleagues referred to me as the 'RGJ Road Runner'.

My replacement was WO1 Tony Jarry, who when interviewed by my colonel he was asked if he could play the piano, stand on the top whilst singing the regimental march and then somersault off!! We all laughed. This was of course an exaggeration. Tony Jarry took my place and was the conductor for twelve years; sadly, he passed away in 2014.

John Warren, Myself and Jeff Hinchliffe.

CHAPTER 28

ROYAL GREEN JACKETS
(60TH RIFLES) –WINCHESTER 1973–1975

Arriving at Winchester—the original capital of England—I could not help admire the training depot. This was the original, intended home of Charles II in 1683, but he died in 1685, and the home was never completed. In 1796, the site was leased from the Crown for use as a military barracks and later officially known as The Rifle Depot.

Walking down the path towards the band room, I could hear music from 'The Sound of Music', and cringed at the bad intonation. This was my promotion. But these were only boys, and it was a training school. There would be a lot of work to help this group. I would now be marching with the band at a speed of 140 paces to the minute, which could have been worse, as the Ghurkha Regiment marched at 160, and I was informed that the KSLI (Kings Shropshire Light Infantry) marched at 180 paces! I think it would have been amusing to watch this spectacle.

My task now was to train young boys aged between fifteen and seventeen years old, and when ready for man's service at seventeen and a half, send them to Regiments in the Light Infantry. I was introduced to my Band Sergeant, WO11 Digger Ashby, who took me to meet the band.

My wife and I moved into a large furnished house, just a five-minute walk from Peninsular Barracks. The children were no longer in boarding school at Sidmouth, and we found new schools close by in Winchester, which they could also walk to. It was a change for all of us. The school was much bigger than what the children had been used to. I no longer had the overseas allowance, plus there would not be the lucrative band engagement money from both concert and dance band. On most days I worked solely on the morning, except for a pass-out parade, which I would be expected to attend. Both Bugle Major Smith and I suffered these long, uneventful parades, until I came up with a unique diversion. At the inspection of the cadets, we turned smartly to the right and marched off behind a building, where I had arranged for a waiter to serve us two large gin and tonics. We had time to enjoy our drink and a cigarette before the inspection finished, with WO11Ashby conducting the band in my absence. The band had very few public engagements, spending most of the time with musical training. I encouraged my musicians to take Royal School of Music graded exams before becoming eligible to join a regiment. I had a list of the instrumentation of all the bands in the light division, and would attempt to keep an instrumental balance for each band. Some of the more talented boys would reach a Grade 8 level, before leaving.

Digger Ashby was a character and his reputation was widely known by everyone. He had different methods of discipline when dealing with the boys. I walked into his office one morning to discover a boy hanging on a coat hook by his collar, while Ashby was giving him a short back and sides. As he finished cutting he said, "Now, next time get a proper haircut, and you won't have to go through this!" I could barely contain my laughter; however, his method worked, and we did not have a repeat of this circus.

There was an occasion when one of the boys had spray painted his army boots with a gold lacquer, just before the band were leaving on a marching tour. Asking

RGJ Road runner – Winchester

Ashby what punishment he had in mind for the boy, he replied: "Wait till we arrive in London, sir. I think you will appreciate this one!" The bus came to a stop; we had arrived and the boys were making their way to the rooms, except for our 'Golden Boot wonder', who was asked to remain on the bus. WO11 Ashby produced a small bucket of water and a toothbrush, and handing them to the boy, he said: "Get cleaning the outside of this bus." The poor boy lasted an hour, but was then relieved and sent to supper.

Struggling financially, I took on some instrumental teaching in two schools during the afternoons. Also, my wife got a job cleaning schools, and both of us got some extra work in a factory during the evenings. I was making kettle elements, and Rosemary was assembling washing machine switches. I can remember saving enough money to buy a bag of coal to heat our big house. We acquired a Bassett hound puppy (Fred) who, when left alone, could be heard howling over a hundred yards away.

I taught bassoon and clarinet at St Swythun's school for girls, or more correctly should I say, a finishing school for young ladies. The fees for boarding were almost £10,000 per term, and £6000 for a day student. At my interview with the headmistress, I was told in very stern terms the conditions of my appointment. "We don't accept failure at the school, and if your student fails an exam, your contract is terminated," she said, staring me down. With this in mind, I was very selective with students sitting Royal Conservatory Examinations.

There was a specialist teacher for almost everything. Both Anglican and Catholic priests were on staff, as were the tennis professionals, volley ball and field hockey positions. In music there was a teacher for each discipline: violin, viola, cello, double bass, brass, myself for bassoon and clarinet, and flute was taught by a local instrumentalist from the city orchestra. There were strict rules for teachers. The door had to remain open, and the lesson was for one hour. A number of the girls were rebellious, and successfully managed to disrupt the system with some of the staff. I was lucky. My students were cooperative, serious about their work, and I had just four pupils to instruct lasting a full year before I left for Canada.

My other private school was St John's preparatory school for boys, some six miles east of Winchester. I taught clarinet and beginner trumpet. I purchased a small scooter to get me to and from the school on a Thursday afternoon. The boys were very polite, respectful and talented. I taught in the dormitory, with two students present all the time. This was a good safeguard for student and teacher, ensuring good teaching practices. There was one time when I was feeling really exhausted and I fell asleep in the middle of a lesson. Two boys let me sleep, bringing me a cup of tea, twenty minutes later. They both promised that they would not say anything about my unprofessional behaviour, but I went to the headmaster's office and explained my predicament; he laughed, and offered me a scotch before I left. That day as I rode home on my scooter, I stood up and sang at the top of my voice, swallowing a fly in the process.

The band went on a recruiting drive to Liverpool, playing in several schools. Some of the areas were in poor districts. In one school, seventy percent of the students came from families surviving on social assistance. At one Catholic school the students behaved badly. During my concert, a boy in the front gave the band the finger. I handed the baton over to Digger Ashby, and went and sat by him. I grabbed his arm, and whispered in his ear, "I wouldn't do that again if I were you." Looking scared, he agreed that this was not acceptable behaviour, and gave me a quick apology.

My posting to the Rifle Depot was a promotion, preparing me for a position as Director of Music. I studied for the psm (passed school of music) exam. There were five parts to this: harmony, aural, instrumentation, conducting and commandants interview. On my first attempt I sat and passed harmony, aural and instrumentation. I returned to take the remaining subjects, but failed. I was disappointed at first but suspected there were other reasons for failing me. It was an old boys' club; could it be due to the fact that I had not joined the Masons? I had been approached several times by different people, but did not think it was for me.

Returning to Winchester, I began drinking heavily. I had to cancel my teaching for the afternoon as a result of my drinking. I was hung over the next morning, arriving late for work, and then be drinking again at noon. I remember staggering home in uniform, and waking up later in the vegetable patch in the garden. This was a time that I would rather forget.

Rehearsing on parade with the bugles one morning, I noticed the face of a small boy looking out the window from the flats opposite the parade ground. Bugle Major Smith and I waved to him. The following day he came to my office and asked if he could watch our parade. Jason Loch was just eight years old, and was born with a weak chest, which meant that one of his lungs would not expand properly. Despite this we invited him for a bugle lesson; he enjoyed it so much that started coming twice a week, which resulted in curing his complaint. Jason's life took a turn for the better, and was now able to join in with games and attend school on a regular basis. I was interviewed on ITV, and was careful not to say that this was a miracle, and that the bugle lessons had helped his lung recover. Both Jason and his parents were convinced that it was a miracle; perhaps it was.

I had become unsettled, and was losing interest in my job. I started looking for a solution, searching for another position out of the Army. There was the chance of applying for a teaching position in Gordonston as a bandmaster. This is an exclusive private school in Moray, Scotland. Three previous generations of British Royalty were educated here. The salary was low, but the job came with a fully furnished house, which was rent-free. Hunting, shooting and fishing were the main attractions in this area, but believing there were other options to consider, I decided not to apply for the position.

Later that month, I was conducting the band in London and working with a fellow bandmaster, Eric Slater, who had just secured a position as a teacher in Canada, and was emigrating when his contract terminated with the British Army.

When I returned to Winchester, I decided to make further enquiries regarding a teaching position in Canada. Eric Slater sent me a letter from Canora, Saskatchewan, where he had been appointed Band Director in a school system, teaching in two schools. He was enjoying the freedom of Canada. Having been there less than three months, he had bought a house and a new car. Life was good and his family were settling into their new way of life.

Queen's regulation 503 – serial 11, states: ". . .at the soldier's request, after completing sixteen or more years on current engagement, discharge will be granted." An added bonus was that with the rank of WO1, I also qualified for a full pension, payable on my sixtieth birthday, plus an untaxed amount of three times the value of my pension. I could retire at age thirty-five and begin a new career; but, before I could make any changes, I had to put my financial affairs in order. Frankly I was in a hopeless mess with money, and had to come up with a solution before I could accept any job offer. I had already sent my résumé to Eric Slater, who had submitted it to a school board in Hudson Bay. I was not chosen for an interview—with the position being offered to a Canadian—and my information was forwarded to Outlook in Saskatchewan. I was unaware of this activity, and was quite shocked when I received a phone call from Canada offering me a position as a band teacher. I was to begin in September. All I had to do was emigrate!

My service of sixteen years, two hundred and thirty six days, had come to an end. Serving her Majesty had been a privileged experience. The British Government paid for my musical training and I had achieved my ambition to become a bandmaster. Once my debts were paid off, I could look forward to another career of teaching in Canada.

CHAPTER 29

MOVING TO SASKATCHEWAN, CANADA (1975)

Having resigned from my position as bandmaster, I now had the task of paying my bills before I could leave the country; this was going to be a difficult task. I went to my local Westminster bank for some advice. Trying to borrow money with no collateral was laughable, so the manager told me. It seemed that I would not be able to accept the position, and I phoned back to Canada explaining my dilemma. The superintendent was sympathetic, and was prepared to give me more time to find a solution.

I decided that I would travel to London, and try borrowing money from a Canadian bank. Getting off the train at Victoria, I had no idea where I would go. I walked off the platform and found a phone box to look up addresses for Canadian banks. I said a quick prayer for help and guidance, opened the phone book and found the Bank of Montreal on Threadneedle Street. Arriving at the bank, I was greeted by a secretary, who enquired what time my appointment was that morning. However, when she discovered that I had no arrangement to see the manager, she suggested that I return in three weeks to speak with him. I informed her that I had travelled ninety miles from Winchester, and would wait to see the manager. She shrugged her shoulders as I sat down to wait. There were four other people with appointments before me, but it was certainly worth a try. Later, as the manager arrived, I could see the secretary talking to him, and looking in my direction. I was invited ahead of everyone, and found myself sitting in his office. "Good morning, Mr. Scholfield, what can I do for you?"

I stammered: "I would like to borrow $10,000, to pay off some debts, and accept a job with the Outlook School Unit No 32 in Saskatchewan." Smiling, he then told me that he had just arrived in London, from Outlook, and was not only familiar with the school district, but knew Peter Popowich— the superintendent—personally! Coincidence, I think not. I showed him my job offer, and after confirming that my salary would be higher in Canada, he said he would consider my request, adding that I had held my last job for sixteen years, which showed stability. I was told that although he could not promise anything, he would make some phone calls and give me his decision in two hours. I left and found a coffee house, anxious for time to pass.

As I entered the bank, I caught sight of the manager behind the teller. He beckoned me over and smiling, told me that the loan had been approved and was in my new account, which he had opened for me. In addition to this he had provisionally booked nine flights with CP Air, pending our immigration papers. I could not believe my good fortune, and was overwhelmed with everything that had passed that morning. The manager had tried to phone my wife with the good news, but decided that it would be better for me to tell her. After signing some papers, he showed me a map of Saskatchewan, wishing me luck with my new future. *Who said God does not answer prayers!* I virtually skipped along the pavement to Victoria Station, when I met my old bank manager (coincidence?), who had just sent me a letter about my overdraught at his bank. I just had to tell him about my morning; the look on his face was one of disbelief, and with a stunned look, shook his head and went on his way.

I had a good feeling about our future. Travelling back to Winchester I was anxious to begin packing our belongings, and tell my wife and family the good news. Living in a furnished Army quarter, was going to make moving a lot easier, having to sell and give away only a few items. I would have to find a good home for Fred our Basset hound. Thoughts were racing through my mind at such speed; I started making a list of things to do before being able to leave England.

Arriving back in Winchester, I celebrated my good fortune with my family; everyone was excited about our forthcoming move to Canada. I ordered a dozen large packing cases, and began preparation for visas for all of us. We were offered free room and board at the Monkton Court Hotel for nine of us. My father-in-law was a generous man. I finished our final packing at the hotel, and was attempting to fit a coffee table into one of the crates, but it was too long. My father-in-law asked me what was so special about it that I needed to take it to Canada. Some years previously, my wife and the band were in a hotel lounge relaxing, when an attractive girl (who was not wearing a bra) walked by, which turned a few heads. My wife commented: "What would you do if I did that?"

"You wouldn't dare," I said.

The bet was on and the price of the challenge was a coffee table she had seen in a store on the high street. A year later at an evening function, my wife went to the ladies' room, removed her bra and paraded before everyone. I bought the table, and now it was a special piece of furniture. However, I had to cut two feet off the end to fit it into the crate. We still have that table.

Arranging a visa to leave the country and qualify for landed immigrant status was a nightmare, with interviews at Canada House, medical examinations, and acquiring court papers, giving permission to take children out of the country, and dealing with bureaucracy. We had particular difficulty finding the whereabouts of the father of my wife's children by her first marriage and there had been no contact or maintenance for several years, but hiring a private detective gave immediate results. I had to also get a court judge to sign papers, which again was delayed because of procedure. Frustrated, I went to a courtroom myself, and persuaded the clerk of the court to get a signature from the judge. I remember the clerk saying to me, "You do realize that his honour is in the middle of a murder trial, don't you!" Our papers were now in order, except for the medical clearance for my eldest son Clive. There seemed to be a problem with a urine test, which was showing a high sugar content. After some arguments, we got a second opinion and the first results were overruled, saying that tests on the urine of adolescent boys cannot be done early in the morning, as they produce false results, and should only be tested after lunch.

Finally, I got the phone call from Canada House that our papers were approved and we would fly out of the UK, arriving at Canada on 8 October in Saskatchewan. I would miss the first month of school, but this was not a problem. We had our farewell parties, packed twenty-six suitcases, hired a van, and left for London Airport.

At the check-in we were told that our luggage was overweight, and we were asked to pay an extra £1000.00! I could not believe this, and we had no alternative than to start unpacking our cases, discarding clothes and anything we could manage without. We had quite an audience watching our performance. After a few minutes, the booking clerk came over to me and said, "If I make it a one hundred pounds, does that sound better?" With a sigh of relief we repacked our bags, and said our goodbyes to family. Both our parents were stood, looking sad and relieved. We would come back to visit, and they could come out to visit us, once we were settled. Lots of hugs, kisses and tears, we then disappeared through security, and on our way to Canada.

My career with OHMS was finally over, leaving with no regrets and a host full of happy memories. Now, I had a chance to sort my life out: get rid of my drinking habit and save my marriage. In addition, I had an opportunity to give my family a better future, and explore a new career in teaching bands in Canadian schools. I did not think I would miss the British Army or my old way of life. This turned out to be the best decision of my life.

Part II

CHAPTER 30

ARRIVING IN CANADA (1975)

Our route was London to Amsterdam with Air Lingus, Amsterdam to Winnipeg with Canadian Pacific, and the last flight of our journey, Winnipeg to Saskatoon with Air Canada. We would then travel to Outlook, Saskatchewan, which would be our final destination. Arriving in Amsterdam, we checked our luggage for Canada and boarded a Canadian Pacific plane. Everyone was excited and soon the children were chatting with some of the passengers. Amanda cut her finger and asked the steward for an 'Elastoplast (Brand name). Shaking his head, he said, "What is that?" with a heavy French accent. A passenger helped, and revealed that what she wanted was a Band-Aid. We would have to re-think our choice of words going to Canada. Car bonnet was hood, boot was trunk, and with a cheeky grin, the steward whispered to me, "Be careful, eraser is not rubber!"

Getting drinking water

We arrived safely in Winnipeg, the port of entry, and first had to go through the immigration offices to receive our landed immigrant status. This was a comedy of errors! Both Rosemary and I had children from our first marriages, and one child from our own marriage. The immigration official could not understand how Malcolm and Sarah were born less than a month apart! After a lot of discussion, all the children took my surname (Scholfield) for passport and immigration purposes; we then had to go through customs. Our next flight was the last plane to Saskatoon that day, and was already being held for us to board. The customs official took one look at our twenty-six suitcases, shook his head and then waved us through. We were greeted on the plane with a loud round of applause and smiles, delaying the plane for twenty minutes. The temperature in Winnipeg was warm for October, and the plane was full. It was Thanksgiving, and families were getting together to celebrate.

As we landed in Saskatoon it was snowing. I thought *Snow in October! This is going to be different.* The superintendent welcomed us, helping with our bags. We had yet to travel another hour and a half to Outlook. Our transport was a school bus, which we needed for nine of us plus our luggage. Looking at the snow falling against the window, I thought to myself, *What have I done? It's too late to turn back now,* and then cheering up, I shared my sense of adventure with the children. My wife just looked at me, smiling and raising her eyebrows.

My plan was to live in two motel rooms for a short while, until I could find suitable rented accommodation for my family. The second day I bought a second-hand Oldsmobile big enough for all of us. I had $1800.00 in the bank and had to find a place quickly. We looked at several places, which were all unsuitable. But after three weeks we found a rental house, furnished in the small town of Elbow, which had a friendly Norwegian community. I had a week to settle, before I was required to teach in school. The first day, local neighbours gave us a TV set, fruit, vegetables and other treats. My rent was $100.00 a month. We would have to wait for our own belongings, which were being shipped from Southampton to Toronto, and then by train to Saskatoon. Expected arrival was January, which would take three months.

Rosemary spent the next while, finding a home for everything, making the place presentable, whilst I began my assignment working in four schools as a band teacher for the Outlook School Unit No 32. In addition to teaching locally in Elbow and Loreburn, I was expected to travel to Beechy and Lucky Lake, which were a good distance away. I would leave at 06:15, travel over the Diefenbaker Dam, arriving in time for assembly, through all weather conditions. Beechy and Lucky Lake were some distance away from my house in Elbow. I was given a gas allowance to help out. All the schools were in small towns, and everyone knew each other. Beechy had a population of 289, and the other towns were even smaller, which was quite a contrast from the population of Winchester.

CHAPTER 31

BEECHY, LUCKY LAKE, LOREBURN AND ELBOW

On my first day travelling, I did not meet any traffic for about ten miles; in fact, I was taken aback by how barren the roads were. Running beside my car was a fox, and the sky was black with geese and ducks flying to warmer calms. I had never experienced anything like this in my life. It was certainly different from my military life back in UK. The band programme in Canada had already been set up by Ronald McCormack, who worked out of Outlook. I was to be his assistant. Ronald was a hard worker, bit of a micro-manager, but had created a good system in the schools. All the schools would get together for a spring concert, and each school would put on a performance at Christmas and school year end in each separate school. The standard of music was poor, few students actually practiced, mediocre seemed to be the norm. I worked in each school, hoping that I would be able to improve things, but needed time to produce any results.

Driving home that night, I saw my first Canadian sunset. It was a wonderful, spiritual moment. It was so incredible, that I stopped my car to look at the red sky. Another motorist pulled up, to ask if I needed help. "Look at that sunset, it's amazing, don't you think?" I said.

"Seen one, seen 'em all," he replied.

By early November I was familiar with the teaching assignment and was enjoying the change from my past military life. My children were getting used to the schools, making new friends and adapting to the Canadian way of life. They had been used to schools with over 1,000 students in Winchester, as compared to 200 at their new school. The travelling back and forth to schools, prompted me to look for a house nearer Beechy and Lucky Lake, with only one day to travel to Loreburn and Elbow. I found a trailer/house in Beechy and got possession in early December. Beechy was another small town, no traffic lights, pavements or street lighting. One hotel, one school, hardware store, café, ice rink, and a population of about 300, who were mostly farmers.

Our new home was basically a trailer, with an unfinished basement; there was a lot of work to be done. There was a propane tank at the back, and the nearest house was the home of the doctor, which was just across a yard. The town doctor was a Scotsman and both of us turned up with our wives at a dance, dressed in full evening attire. Everyone else was in a cowboy shirt and jeans! We never did that again. One evening the doctor invited himself to our house, sat at the kitchen table with a bottle of single malt scotch. He had been through a bad day, and shared his frustrations with me. We finished the bottle, and retired to the local hotel, drinking some beer and introduced the game of knuckles to the locals. It was a lot of fun, and the following day there were lots of men walking round with bruised knuckles. Dr. Tennant was six-foot three and weighed 230 pounds. He had a shock of black hair and bushy eyebrows, which made him look like a bear.

The following week, I received a letter informing me of the arrival of my packing cases from UK. I would have to drive to Saskatoon to pick them up. A teacher, who had a truck, offered to drive me to collect the cases. We arrived in Saskatoon, loaded everything, and made our way back to Beechy in a fierce snowstorm. I was a little anxious as the road seemed to disappear, but my companion just laughed, telling me that it was only a *white out*, quite common on the prairies, but not recommended to drive in these conditions. However, driving at a slow speed, we limped home and arrived safely. My eldest son Clive was with us to help with the loading. We were tired from the journey and decided to go to bed, leaving the unpacking until the following morning.

Waking up the following day, my son rushed into my bedroom yelling, "The truck has been stolen!" Looking out the window there was no sign of our truck, but when I stepped outside, I could see the truck with our cases at the bottom of the hill. The sheer weight on the truck had caused it to roll down the hill, striking nothing and coming to rest in a snow bank.

The children had asked if we could get a dog, and I started looking in the paper for a dog needing a good home. I found an advert for an English Sheepdog, which was free, and was to be picked up in Regina, a good distance away. Arriving at the address, we were introduced to Mr. Mugs, a beautiful two-year-old with lots of energy. He was friendly, liked children, and was free. Having collected his collar, leads, bowls and toys, we were about to leave when his owner said, "Now, we should settle the deal and complete the financial paperwork."

I looked at him in horror: "But the dog was free," I spluttered. We discovered that there had been an error in the advert and the asking price had been $300.00. I could not afford to pay this, but looking at the kids' faces, I had little choice but to write him out a cheque, which meant that I was going into my overdraught. We drove home in our Delta 98, Oldsmobile, with Mr. Mugs sat in the back, licking faces and sprawling over the children.

After my experience with the Bank of Montreal in London, England, my faith had become stronger. We attended church each Sunday, which was in walking distance from our home. Father Paul Donlevy, a newly appointed priest was the pastor, serving four additional towns: Elrose, Forgan, Kyle and Lucky Lake. Often, we would find him asleep in his car between towns. Father Paul became a close family friend, with a great sense of humour and lots of energy. He arranged a lobster supper with wine in the church basement as a fundraiser for the Parish, planning to have the lobster flown in from the east for the occasion. He suggested that our committee should have a rehearsal the week before, but the lobster was stolen at the airport.

The supper night arrived; we had sold most of the tickets, and I was in charge of the wine. Our party was well underway when a hunting party of twenty asked to join us. We had plenty of food, and wine. I sold all the wine, most of it to the hunting party. Our evening was an outstanding success, so successful that the Bishop of Saskatoon wanted to know how we made over $1000.00 profit in one evening. I told him to make sure he invited a hunting party.

After a long battle with a chronic illness, Father Paul passed away in 2011. His openness, honesty, humour, integrity will be remembered by many. *Father Paul, we miss you.*

I was enjoying my teaching and had already had some success with raising the standards in the school bands, forming a joint honour band from students in Lucky Lake and Beechy High School. I had entered the band into the 'Moose Jaw Music' competition, where there would be many good bands from the States competing. Suddenly my world was shattered. I received a letter from the Department of Education, who were reducing my salary. My professional certificate could not be granted, and I was to receive a standard grading, which not only reduced my salary, it would leave me in a financial mess. The school board and superintendent were not interested in helping. The Department of Education did not recognize my qualification from the London School of Music, which prompted me to write a letter to the Ombudsman in Saskatchewan, who agreed that I had been treated unjustly and he would begin an investigation.

Several months passed without any news, when six months later I received a letter informing me that my qualifications were in order, and that a professional certificate had been issued on a retroactive basis, dated 1 September 1975. Winning the day with the Department of Education and the University of Saskatchewan was extremely gratifying, and I have only the Ombudsman to thank for his efficient investigation at a ministerial level. There were a lot of embarrassed faces at the next school board meeting,

Returning to the truck incident with our boxes, I had arranged to drive back to Elbow to join my family for a New Year's Eve party, which my neighbour was throwing. The RCMP at the foot of the Diefenbaker Dam stopped me; the bridge was closed. Explaining my dilemma, the officer showed me how to drive across the ice to the other side. This was certainly a new experience for me. I arrived in time to bring in the New Year with my family. My neighbour had set up chairs in his garage with heaters to combat the freezing weather. One by one the children fell asleep in their sleeping bags while we waited for the stroke of midnight, bringing in a New Year, our first in Canada.

The dress code in Canada was so much more relaxed than what I had been used to in England, where I would not think of attending any function without a suit and tie. It did not take me long to dress casual, and for me it was so much more comfortable. No more ties! My teaching was rewarding, with small classes of polite students, whom I had a lot of fun with. I asked a class of grade 9 girls if anyone could give me a *rubber!* Not realizing the implication behind the remark, I made it worse by adding: "Surely, someone in the class has a rubber?" The whole class had a good chuckle, informing me that the term was eraser, not rubber!

I had been encouraged to buy the trailer in Beechy, which later I found was grossly overpriced. An unscrupulous man in Beechy, none other than the Mayor, led me like a lamb to the slaughter. With my recent salary cut—despite the retroactive payment—I was struggling to pay my bills. It was at this time that my wife's parents were going to visit us from England, which could not have been at a worse time. To free up some cash, I traded my new Oldsmobile for a second-hand AMC Pacer. My father-in-law was not impressed with my choice, but I was too proud to explain my reasons for the switch. To make matters worse, my in-laws wanted to travel to the mountains and I could not let them use the Pacer. Father Paul came to my rescue and offered his roomy ford for them to travel. My mother in-law was not feeling well during her visit, and it was later that we learned she had cancer. I often wonder what they must of thought, visiting us in our little run down trailer, when they were used to a different lifestyle that offered all the home comforts.

CHAPTER 32

MOVE TO PRINCE ALBERT

The one thing that I really missed from the UK was the presence of trees, which were non-existent on the southern prairies. Looking at the map, I noticed further north was a different landscape, abundant with trees. Prince Albert, Saskatchewan was some 320 kilometres from Beechy, and had several schools in the district. Looking in the paper, there was a job for a band teacher in the Roman Catholic School system. It was Sunday, however, I phoned the number of the office, and luckily the superintendent answered the call. He came to meet me, and thirty minutes later I had signed a contract to begin a school band programme that year.

Returning to Beechy, I resigned that morning, and began packing up yet again. I was worried about money, but managed to secure a house for my family, hoping for better things in the coming year.

Day by day, trying to pay off bills and remain solvent was becoming more difficult, and after some finance counselling, it was recommended that I declare personal bankruptcy. My lawyer was a school board member who helped me through this difficult time. We joined the Parish of St Joseph, where I began to play the organ for the service, and made new friends from the church and school. My new job was exciting and interesting, as I formed the first band at a new school called Holy Cross. I also taught in two other schools, St Mary High School and Boucher Junior High.

The Staff at Holy Cross were friendly and supportive to one another, giving gifts at Christmas time, and holding year-end parties. There was a new Industrial Arts teacher appointed after the sad passing away of Tony Drescher. We had just exchanged our gifts—which were traditionally 'joke' presents—when the staffroom door opened and our new Director of Education came in to shake hands with everyone. Barry—our new teacher—was holding his gift (a plastic penis, from a banana) in his right hand, and then quickly moved the offensive banana to his left hand, shaking hands with the director, who had a stunned look on his face.

At this time the charismatic renewal movement was growing in our church; both Rosemary and I joined this group attending meetings at the church each week. Some months later I received a call from a parishioner, who wanted us to get together with others and pray for a healing. Her son had a large swelling on his right foot. I looked on as ten parishioners laid their hands on the boy, and the swelling on his foot disappeared before our eyes. *It was amazing!* There were a lot of tears and thanks to God. If I had not been present at this miracle, I doubt that I would have believed. This really strengthened my faith.

After my first month of working as an Itinerant Band Teacher for the Separate System, some senior teachers, asked me to consider joining the Knights of Columbus, a Catholic fraternal organization. There were many teachers who were Knights and although I was not overly keen to join I accepted the invitation. New candidates were told to meet in the school assembling in the staffroom in preparation for the initiation ceremony, 'Riding the Goat'. About forty of us were crammed into the room, feeling uncomfortable, and complaining about the heat. After an hour of waiting, our patience was wearing thin, and a heated argument erupted between two candidates, one of whom was a priest. I could smell booze on the candidate who looked as though he was going to hit the priest, but we were all called to assemble in the Rotunda with hoods placed on our heads, allowing us limited vision through the eye slots.

The ceremony began with the Grandmaster asking personal questions to several of the candidates. The drunk in our midst started arguing again with the priest and became aggressive, making a move to hit him. I intervened by blocking his arm and it was then that I realized we were being tested for a reaction. The candidates had been set up. The heat had been purposely turned up in the staff room; the (fake) drunk and the priest were already Knights, and we had 'Ridden the Goat'. The ceremony concluded with a laying on of hands on a skull, repeating a sacred oath, and finally we were congratulated as having passed the test and were now officially Knights of the first and third degree.

I went to a few meetings over the next three months, paid my dues, and was impressed with the charitable work that the Knights took on, fundraising for good causes; however the group that I had joined seemed to be more interested in drinking after a short meeting, and my interest dwindled and finally, I let my membership lapse. I have not returned since that time.

Declaring bankruptcy was both humiliating and embarrassing, yet we both had a feeling of relief that the debts hanging over us were now removed. It was a chance to start over again and to re-establish our credit; still, with seven children, our progress was going to be slow. My philosophy was to keep a stiff upper lip and carry on, into the next wall!

A year passed and we were discharged from our bankruptcy and attempted to re-establish our credit. Returning home from church one Sunday, we received a distressing phone call from Charles, my father in-law. Peggy was dying from cancer, and only had a short time to live. Rosemary and I discussed what we could do, when we decided to sell our home and take the entire family home with the proceeds. A real estate friend agreed to sell my house, and gave me the equivalent equity to make our trip possible.

I placed our belongings in storage, booked our flights, and returned to England to spend six memorable weeks with Peggy. She was able to spend time with the children, walking along the seafront at Sidmouth and going out for tea. This was a very peaceful time for everyone.

On returning to Canada, we rented a house and started again. Two months later we received news that Peggy had passed away, and made arrangements for Rosemary and our eldest daughter Amanda, to go to her funeral.

I was able to buy another house that needed some work, but would be better than renting. The basement was unfinished and with help we added some bedrooms for the children.

The new Catholic school, Holy Cross, was due to open, and I was asked to provide suitable music for the occasion. I had only a few students to draw from, but managed to produce a fanfare for the opening ceremonies. Prior to the building of Holy Cross, all teachers were asked for input with regard to the design. I had asked for a larger door for the instrument room, which would let us take the timpani through. The door worked fine, but the architect forgot about the entrance door to the band room. The land, which the school was built on, was acquired at a cheap price, but a year later I learnt that originally this was swampland. The ground was shifting, and doors and cupboards were hard to close. The school was built in the shape of a cross, which could be seen only from above. There was to be no landscaping until the following year, and the school was surrounded with mud, which the students would tread through the building—the school was carpeted throughout. Our Principal was Chris Farthing, who was young, full of energy, and very supportive to the teachers. The students were mainly from well-off families and spoilt. Discipline was non-existent in some classes, but not in mine. I had one class of grade 7 students, who had difficulty with walking into a room and sitting on a chair. My room was a band room, without desks, and the students would run into the room fighting over chairs. My solution was to line them up and march them into the room in silence; it took three classes before they got the message that I was the adult in charge. Chairs were in four different colours. I would get them to stack, and then restack the chairs, trying every combination possible, until I was satisfied.

Success came the third week, and the behaviour was much improved. Once in my music class I caught a boy drinking a slush, which he had hidden under his jacket. I stood behind him, grabbed the drink, and dumped it on his head. Returning to my class, having cleaned himself up, he was made to apologize. I never had another student bring a drink into my class. This was good old-fashioned discipline. Try this today, and you would lose your job. There were incidents of unruly behaviour throughout the school, and in such cases, the culprits were dealt with. Nevertheless, teaching was so much fun in those days, enjoying the students, learning and having fun.

The Roman Catholic School Division had hired me to introduce a new band programme in three schools: St Mary's High School, and two junior high schools. I had the task of purchasing instruments for the students, sending out a list of our requirements to several music companies. A local music shop, Gordie Brandt's, gave a very reasonable quote and their tender was accepted. The proprietor was Hal Turner, who supplied all our needs for the new programme, giving generous discounts on instruments and helping with advice about the best brands to buy. Hal had a great sense of humour and liked to play practical jokes on his customers, always striking when you least expected it. Hal had made a delivery of instruments to Holy Cross School, leaving several boxes in the band room. Climbing into an empty tuba box, waiting for the band to start playing, he made animal noises to attract our attention. Thinking there was a dog in the room we stopped playing, until he finally leapt from the box with a big grin on his face. After this prank, I vowed that I would return the compliment, warning him that I would strike at any time.

Dave Monette, a colleague of mine, who taught band at P.A.C.I. (Prince Albert Collegiate Institute), suggested that we hold up the store one Thursday evening when the shop was busy. We arrived at the store armed with toy guns and stockings and burst through the front door, ordering customers to stand against the wall. The result was really quite stunning, as Hal and terrified customers raised their hands. After realizing that this was all a prank. Hal left Prince Albert, and is now working in Real Estate in Saskatoon; shortly after his departure the store closed down.

I became involved with Jack Cennon, a broadcaster for CKBI and Cec Corrigal, who owned a local fur shop; both these characters were recovering alcoholics, and were the key organizers for the Spring Roundup in Prince Albert. I was hired as a piano player for their weekly choir practice in preparation for a final concert at the end of the roundup. The choir was always in good form, singing with lots of spirit (the non-liquid type), liveliness, bravado and gusto. I always enjoyed these rehearsals, working the choir as hard as I dare, getting them ready for the final performance. Both Jack and Cec were helpful organizing the programme, with Cec making sure the choir would sing 'God Bless America' as the finale. After drinking a few beers with my son Malcolm at the Legion, I arrived late at one rehearsal and made every attempt to disguise the smell of alcohol. Nobody said anything to me, but I don't think I fooled anyone, despite my excellent boisterous piano playing.

Boucher Junior High School was one of the three schools I had to teach in. This school was styled on a different system, where students worked at their own speed, completing blocks of work in an open area. There was a relaxed atmosphere in the school, although I am not sure this was the best for learning. I do remember seeing three students—who had obviously behaved badly—kneeling in the hall, with their noses against the wall, and their arms stretched out with heavy books in each hand. I would think this was close to torture! The teacher Peter Reiss, however, begged to differ, and believed this was a suitable punishment.

St Mary's High School was the last of my assignments. Having been kicked out of the original room due to the noise, the band room was in the basement. The school had good discipline, a strong Principal and a mature staff. I had a great time with my senior students, although few took music as a serious subject and treated it as an easy credit. I smoked a pipe at that time, and had left it on my music stand. Later, when I lit up, I almost choked. Students had filled the bowl with marijuana! I returned the compliment by handing out a university exam paper as a test for my grade 10 class. The look on their faces was one of horror, until they saw me smiling and realized this was payback time.

There are always people who you meet in life that you never forget; they might upset you, make you laugh, perhaps influence you . . . or you just like being around them. My story would be incomplete without including Louis Doderai, a fellow teacher at Holy Cross Junior High School, who was and still is a good friend—and troublemaker! He played several pranks on me during my time as a teacher, and one always had to be on their guard, as you never knew when he was going to strike. At a Catholic School Trustees Convention—with nuns present—he placed a condom in an envelope with my name on it, and then dropped it on the floor, which a nun picked up and handed it to me. We played numerous pranks on each other—and everybody else—including walking downtown dressed as tramps, and he even created a phony scenario that involved me believing that I was a bad influence and had to move to another Parish. I should have guessed that one to be a fake, but I fell for it, nevertheless. However, I managed to pay him back, by hiding his entire religion class in the furnace room, while he panicked trying to find them.

We both disagreed with the honour and award system at the school; it was always the same clever students that went home with the certificates and awards. We managed to get hold of the awards, and listed some students that were not that clever, and never received anything. It was amusing to watch the looks of astonishment on the faces of these students, as their names were called out for excellent work. Louis now lives in Saskatoon, coping with a form of Parkinson's disease, but still has his sense of humour, and I know he is still up to his pranks. *Love ya' Louis, don't ever change.*

One of my students, Raelyn, suffered with muscular dystrophy, and was confined to a wheelchair. When I was at Holy Cross School, she would ask me to teach her how to play the piano. My free time was limited to my lunch hour, and I would often use this time to travel to other schools to prepare for the afternoon. Finally, I gave in to her persistence, munching on a sandwich and helping her twice a week; after a few sessions she managed to lift her hands to the keyboard, playing a simplified version of 'Frere Jacque'. She had pins in her arm and back, yet managed to place her fingers on the correct keys, moaning and grinning with pleasure as the tune took shape. Raelyn was invited as our guest artist at the next school concert, playing to an astonished audience; there wasn't a dry eye in the house. Raelyn lived for one more year before she sadly passed away at the age of thirteen.

During the school year there were workshops given by visiting clinicians and priests. The school was assembled for a talk on world poverty, illustrated with fifty slides of people struggling to survive from day to day and living in shocking conditions. As the lecture began, there was a problem with the sound for the slides, and after repeated attempts to correct things, the priest had to stop the presentation. He asked if I could play some music to accompany the pictures on screen, and I suggested the vibraphone would be suitable, pulling it out from the band room. I just looked at the slides and played the appropriate music to fit what I saw. It was a great success, with a silence throughout the slide presentation, causing some students to cry with emotion. The priest was amazed at my effective improvisations, asking me if I could accompany him to the next two schools in the area. I responded that I could never repeat the identical playing, only a similar rendition; however, I could not leave the school as I had teaching commitments for the remainder of the day.

There were several amusing events at Holy Cross during my stay, which reflected the light-hearted spirit amongst the staff, who would tease one another with pranks, particularly at parent teacher interviews. One time the school was full of parents, milling about in the rotunda, waiting their turn to see a teacher. I rushed out from my band room, clutching a guitar, smashing it against the walls, screaming: "I can't take it anymore," to the look of horror on the parents' faces. My guitar was an old broken relic, which I would glue back together for each performance.

During the school year, teachers were expected to attend religious in-services, at which the Bishop of Prince Albert would be in attendance to celebrate mass at the conclusion of the presentation. I found his clerical attire, complete with hat in the Principal's office and could not resist the temptation of wearing the hat; as I stood there, the Bishop came in the office, but only responded with a smile as I hurriedly took off the hat.

Playing organ for weddings and funerals, I met Msgr. Edmund Ulinski, a priest from Poland who had a powerful tenor voice and loved to sing. Edmund lived out his faith by giving money to the poor, letting those who had just been released from jail use his home and bed, bringing refugees over to Canada, starting a food bank, building a new church in Birch Hills, sharing the facility with the Anglican church . . . and much more. He possessed a double doctorate and had suffered as a prisoner of war, some of it at Buchenwald and Bergen-Belsen during WWII. He had spent ten years working at the Vatican, served in many parishes, and held monthly dinners at his modest rectory. He would deliberately invite parishioners from various churches to sit at dinner, while challenging their faith.

Ulinski preached the equality of all people, without discrimination. We would meet to share music, and he would sing a variety of songs, ranging from Bach to his favourite Polish songs. I believe that he was a bit of a thorn in the side of Blaise the Bishop of Prince Albert, mainly because of his outspoken opinions and sermons, which were always getting him into trouble. I can remember him turning up at my house to sing, greeting me with his outstretched arms, he said, "Here I am, Lord." I played for several Polish services for him, and we gave a musical performance at St. Michael's Church one evening, at which the Bishop was sat in the front row. Knowing that these two did not really see eye to eye over certain church matters, I took the opportunity to have some fun. Msgr. was singing a collection of Polish songs, and I announced to the audience that it might be helpful if I gave a small translation about the song. I said, "In English, a loose translation of this piece would be, 'I hate the Bishop, I hate the Bishop!'" Our audience, laughed, and even the Bishop had a smile on his face. Msgr. suffered with deafness, yet he still managed to sing at many functions, with the use of a hearing aid, which he rarely had turned on. On one occasion he came to St Michael's Parish, sitting next to a parishioner who was blind, who had never met him before. As I began the opening hymn, I saw Msgr. sharing a book with our blind friend; we laughed at the thought of the "Deaf showing the blind".

Our friendship ended when I left Prince Albert to teach in Sherwood Park, and was told that Msgr. seemed lost without his weekly singing practice. He finally returned to Poland in 2003 to be with his sister, yet sadly at the age of eighty-three, he died in April of that year. He was missed by many.

My wife was hired at Holy Cross as a librarian, which helped raising our large family. Surviving after our discharge from bankruptcy, I had two old cars: a Chevy Biscayne and a Rambler. Returning home from school one afternoon, I found the Rambler completely dismantled in my back garden. Our son Clive had taken everything apart, but assured me he could put it all back together again. The following day the car was back in one piece, except a few parts, which he assured me were not important. To my amazement the car started. Clive had applied to join the British Army as a boy soldier and was waiting for his papers to join a unit in the UK.

At our weekly prayer meeting we were invited to travel to Minneapolis in the summer to spend time with another family, who belonged to a prayer group called 'Servants of the Light'. We planned to drive from Prince Albert to Minneapolis in the Chevy Biscayne, with nine of us in the car. Before the journey I said a quick prayer for a safe journey as I splashed some holy water over the hood. We made the trip, arriving safely and spent a week with a young American family, who welcomed us into their home and took us to prayer meetings. The 'Servants of the Light', was a highly organized group, with their own real estate company, which moved families from Grand Forks and area to locations in Minneapolis. The extent of their control was really frightening, with restaurants, banks, and even a school which they ran. There was a pecking order of seniority, with males making all the decisions.

At the prayer meeting there was a huge swing band of fourteen players, setting the atmosphere for the evening. I got up to speak at the meeting, and was told politely to sit down. This was a powerful group, and had the notion that it was in this city that the Holy Spirit operated, *and nowhere else!* We enjoyed our stay, which had been a learning experience for both Rosemary and myself. On our return journey of 1,000 kilometres to Prince Albert, there was a heat wave, which resulted in cars overheating. I had a small linkage problem, which I managed to fix temporarily, and we arrived back safely.

The car had given us no problems, but with over 240,000 kilometres on the dial, it was time to get rid of it. I decided to give the car away to a young student who was struggling. He drove off and had the car for two months, before the engine seized.

Prince Albert was a small city of 35,000 people, with a penitentiary and a paper mill, both situated outside the main town. We made monthly trips to Saskatoon where there were a bigger variety of shops and places to visit. On one such trip we stopped for breakfast at a café just outside Saskatoon. When we continued on our journey, my stomach started to ache, and it soon became necessary for me to use the washroom. Having located a garage I rushed to the bathroom. When I returned to the car Alex said that there was an unpleasant smell coming from my body. This was followed by various other episodes of 'stomach attack', which albeit embarrassing in many ways, caused much hilarity.

I received a phone call from my mother to say that my father was sick and had been placed in a home, which was necessary as she could not look after him as she had broken her hip. I was granted compassionate leave of absence of six weeks, with full pay. Arriving in England, my brother and I had to deal with the situation. My mother had returned home and was making an excellent recovery; however, my father was in a poor nursing home, suffering from Parkinson's disease. He was heavily drugged, and did not recognize either of his two sons. We planned for him to be taken off the drugs for a weekend.

When we returned to visit him, he was a different person; father was chatting to us while smoking a manikin cigar and enjoying a small glass of single malt scotch. He asked us when he would be returning home. One of the male nurses had taken his watch, and was wearing a tie I had given him that year as a gift. This sort of elder abuse goes on even today, and makes me not want to ever have to go into a home; hopefully, I will last at home before my time comes.

We moved our father out of this ghastly place and had him placed in a better facility, and recovered his watch and tie before leaving. I will always remember the look on my father's face as I left; I felt guilty about leaving England, and thought I should be helping with things for my parents. However, my brother seemed to have everything under control, keeping his eye on them and attending to their needs.

Arriving back in Canada, I was told that my father had passed away, and was granted another six weeks leave to attend the funeral and help my mother. The Roman Catholic School Board was very understanding and generous with granting me more leave, although I am sure Father Cliff Tremblay made this decision.

Arriving in the UK, I was met by my brother John, who drove me to our parents' house, where we made funeral arrangements. Father had suffered with angina for the past ten years and further complicated with Parkinson's disease. After several massive heart attacks, he gave up and finally found some peace. Mother was totally distraught, and having been so close to our father, she would need some time to recover from the loss.

At the funeral there were a large number of women who came to pay their last respects, as our father had always been the perfect gentleman, giving up his seat on the bus, and treating all ladies with a sincere respect. I hired a car, and took mother to some of the places we had gone to as a family, which eased her pain; in fact, the trip down memory lane cheered her up, and got her laughing at some of the things we had done. Our mother did recover and busied herself in many activities during the following year, canvassing for cancer, active in the local women's guild, and inviting grandchildren for tea. I returned to Canada in the sixth week, knowing that our mother would survive.

I continued teaching at the three schools, and had some help with teaching band at Boucher School. Keith Barrs was my assistant, which enabled me to concentrate on the other two schools. The programme was growing each term and developing into decent sounding bands, especially at the high school. Keith and I staged a religious musical entitled 'The Prodigal Son', between the two junior high schools. Rehearsals were during the lunch hours at Boucher School. We put in a lot of hard work and a very successful show to an audience of delighted parents.

A week later I was summoned to the office of our new personnel director, who was already unpopular with her manner with staff. As I walked into her office I could see my two Principals stood behind her, looking sheepish. I was accused of not keeping to the curriculum, not getting permission to stage this musical, and poor attendance at staff meetings. It

was a pathetic attempt to intimidate me. I then proceeded
to intimidate all three of them, with good effect. My parting
words were: "The interview is over, and my resignation is on
your desk."

CHAPTER 33

PRIVATE TEACHING AND POLITICS

It was 1981 when I set up my private music practice, renting a second floor studio on Main Street in Prince Albert. Within two months, I had over sixty students coming for weekly lessons. My working hours changed, and were now from 15:00–21:00 hours, five days a week. I became interested in politics and put my name forward as a candidate for the Liberal Party, and won the nomination for the Prince Albert Duck Lake Riding. I went to my first meeting with the executive committee in the office of Peter Abramatz, who was a local lawyer and a staunch Liberal. Running for the Liberal Party in Prince Albert Saskatchewan, can only be compared with being a young Conservative in Moscow! There was no chance of winning, but it might have been possible to put a dent in the majority vote for the Tories and NDP.

The reaction from my family was mixed, although they were not sure what had made me make this decision to get involved in politics. I was working with two other candidates, Bill Nutting and Jack Greening, who were also novices at the political game. My business manager, Jim Comiskey, was a fellow teacher; he accompanied me on my door knocking campaigns, which produced a variety of reactions from the public. I had doors slammed in my face, attacked by a dog, invited in for tea, stood arguing on a door step, and physically run off the premises with shouts of "Don't come back (*with a few adjectives!*)."

At every election, there is always a taboo topic that rears its ugly head. In this election the topic for all politicians was the abortion issue, which politicians were told to sidestep and be non-committal with regard to which view they supported. I spoke up about my views, and declared as a Roman Catholic that abortion was murder. My comments not only made the paper, but I received a scolding from Ralph Goodale, the only Liberal in Saskatchewan. Part of my riding was Duck Lake, where there was an Indian Reserve and represented a good chunk of the vote. I arrived in a large white van covered with Liberal slogans—and my own kids hiding out of sight—and ventured into the local hotel bar where I was greeted by a group of local native Indians who were well pissed on a Saturday afternoon. I handed out my election pamphlets, which were torn in two pieces, so decided to make a digni-fied exit. Walking slowly and upright, I could feel the prickles on my neck, but did not look back as I tripped and fell to an outburst of drunken laughter, then running to my van and driving away out of the reserve.

One evening I was knocking on the door of an apartment, which was answered by an elderly man with a nasty bruise on his face, which he suffered as he had fallen down the stairs that morning. He invited me in, and shared some tea with me, talking about his wife who had passed away that year, and his daughter and son, who were too busy to visit him. The poor man was lonely, and wanted some company. I stayed for over an hour, chatting and listening. Walking back home, I gave some thought to my last visit, and realized that there were a lot of lonely people like him who were not interested in politics, and just wanted some company.

My statement about the abortion issue gave me a host full of votes from the nuns at the Riviera Academy in town. The Tories won over half the popular vote, having a majority for the first time in Saskatchewan, taking the power away from the NDP, who had been in control for years with Alan Blakely. Jerry Hammersmith, the Federal MLA, invited me to breakfast, suggesting that I should ask the nuns who voted for me to change to the NDP, which could mean that I could be considered for a position in Education, should the NDP become elected.

Now the Government was going to be led by Grant Divine, who was later defeated after corruption charges were proven, with politicians serving jail time for their unprofessional behaviour. I enjoyed my brief time in politics, met a lot of interesting people, and managed to gain 404 votes, the most of any Liberal candidate in Saskatchewan! Except Ralph Goodale.

CHAPTER 34

PELICAN NARROWS

By the fall of 1982, my political career was over, which allowed me to concentrate on building my music studio. I was having poor attendance from some students, and was losing money each month, when I saw an advert for a music teacher on an Indian Reserve in Pelican Narrows. I applied for the position, went for an interview and was offered the job. Discussing the situation with my wife, we decided that I would go alone, and get back at weekends when I could. There was a Greyhound bus service that ran the 384 kilometres; leaving on a Sunday, it connected with a small bus service to the Reserve.

I had decided to take my car for the first few weeks, trying the unpaved road on the Hanson Lake Highway, with stretches eighty kilometres or more without any services. I arrived and was taken to my lodgings, which was a two-bedroom bungalow, situated on the edge of the town, near the ice arena. I would be sharing with another male teacher from Vancouver. Population of Pelican was 1,600, living in a small town, without running water. Some of the houses—including mine—had water-holding tanks, which worked fine as long as you had quick showers, to avoid running out before the next delivery.

My roommate was Bob Minor, who was teaching Math and English. He was an intellectual with Marxist views, played the violin, drank sherry and had a passion for opera and classical music. My first meeting with Bob consisted of sharing a bit about each other, drinking some dry sherry, and playing 'Dear little Buttercup', from HMS Pinafore.

The school was run down, with bars and boards on the windows at night, and a small gymnasium that smelt like a thousand washrooms. My teaching assignment was K-12, introducing music with singing and some guitar, plus helping teachers with music classes. I created my own curriculum and held morning assemblies encouraging kids to sing. I had a portable keyboard, which I took to each classroom, using simple tunes, religious music and action songs, I soon had everyone hooked on music. I formed a Grade 5/6 choir. And after getting an elder in the town to translate 'O Canada into Cree', rehearsed and entered the choir into the Prince Albert Music Festival singing in the National Anthem Class. We could not lose and came first in a class of one entrant. The kids sang holding big smiles, almost shouting the words with their enthusiasm, everyone enjoyed the moment.

I was working hard and, with little time off, I was granted a four-day week to encourage me to continue. Expecting a change in my pay, I was surprized when my next cheque showed no change, and was told that I was worth it! The kids smelt of smoke from the fires in their homes. I bought toothbrushes for my grade 3 class to introduce them to oral hygiene. After lunch one afternoon, one of my thirteen-year-old students, returned from home drunk, where her parents were drinking on a two-day binge. I slung her over my shoulder, and took her to the nursing station where she could get some help. There were other cases involving young teenagers caught up in domestic issues. Most involved their parents who depended on alcohol, and I was witness to family feuds, with people hurling rocks and yelling at each other. This was the state of things on this Reserve, but the situation did improve as the year went by.

Flin Flon was the nearest town; around 121 kilometres from Pelican, it offered more shops and restaurants. Because of the landscape being bedrock, all the buildings and pipes were raised above ground level, which gave an odd appearance. It seemed on my two visits that there were a lot of people with red hair!

Back in Pelican, I overheard some students talking about the sex show on TV the previous evening, and decided to investigate what was going on. It transpired that the Reserve had a TV dish, which was pointed towards the porn channels. The staff had this changed the next day, after challenging a very embarrassed board chairman, who repeatedly denied any involvement with the dish. Realizing that the dish could be controlled, I launched a plan to film the school in action in the hope that parents might be persuaded to come to parent/teacher interviews. I created an extravagant musical play involving most of the school, with students performing my fairy story, some singing, some dancing, and some dressed as trees and animals. We all had a lot of fun performing this, and it had the desired effect, with parents at home watching their kids on TV, and later visiting the school.

Thanksgiving arrived, and I drove the long journey home through the multi-coloured landscape, with the trees waiting to shed their leaves. I planned to leave my car in Prince Albert so that my wife had some transport, and use the public transport to get back to Pelican. I had also been offered rides from the Reserve from truck drivers and also a free flight from one of the pilots, when they were making that trip on a Thursday afternoon. Returning to Pelican by Greyhound, I was asked to chaperone a young nursing student who was going to Sandy Bay, one stop before Pelican. Her father was a colleague of mine and was a little anxious for the safety of his daughter. She was a bright young lady, and despite her innocent demeanour, was well able to look after herself. Several other teachers from PA used the bus on occasion, which ran in all weathers, taking the stress away from driving themselves.

On one occasion I borrowed a car from a teacher, driving home to Prince Albert to see my family. On my return, the car broke down on the Hansen Lake road about sixty miles from any town or help. It was February, bitterly cold, late at night, and I was worried about survival. Having no blanket, torch, or phone, I was not prepared. After fifteen minutes I saw the headlights of a car travelling towards me, which stopped to help me. The driver was a going to Pelican and helped me move my things into his car. I reported the whereabouts of the car to the RCMP, who informed me that when they found the vehicle, the tires and battery had been taken.

Arriving back in Pelican, I now had to start working on the Christmas concert, where each class would be performing, plus my choirs and some guitar pieces. I coached each class, helping, and advising what they should do. One Grade 4 class had each made a rocking horse (horse's head on a pole) and were moving to music. As I passed the classroom they were in action, and I heard the teacher say, "No, no, you are supposed to be bucking," with a heavy Cree accent. I rushed into the classroom in disbelief; I thought she had said something else! Grade 3 and Grade 4 formed the junior choir, and I taught them a number of catchy tunes, one of which was 'I wish I were a Butterfly'. I managed to get my group to sing with a British accent, whilst they taught me how to announce the song with a Cree accent, bringing spontaneous applause from our audience. Our Christmas concert was a huge success, bringing school and community together, something that had been sadly lacking in previous years.

Living conditions on the reserve were appalling with no running water, poor heating, lack of space, and children sleeping on the floor. In February I saw an elderly man pass my house with two buckets and an axe, on his way to the river to get some fresh water. The school was too small and in a dilapidated state with need of major repairs. Government funding for a new school was proposed, and although conditionally accepted, was going to be a long time before this actually happened, if in indeed at all. Bob and I were joking, saying that the best thing to do was to have a fire; the school would have to be rebuilt. That very evening, we caught some students with paper, wood and matches. They were about to follow through, however, we managed to stop what would have been arson. The phrase: "Be careful what you wish for," came to mind.

The group of teaching staff were mainly younger people; some were running away from a past, while others were just unable to get a job elsewhere in the city, leaving those—including myself—who needed the money. I was earning $50,000, which was a good salary at that time, plus I was able to teach a university class in the evenings, which brought in extra cash needed to pay for our daughter's wedding in the spring. I had arranged to get a lift with the Chief, Joe Custer, who was travelling to Bear Lake, where my wife could meet me and continue back to PA. I was in a white van with six Indians when I saw my wife pass us from the opposite direction. The driver turned our van around to catch up with her but as we were getting closer, she accelerated faster, eventually pulling into a farmyard and hiding under the dash. She had not seen me and thought she was being chased by a van full of unfriendly Indians.

The Chief discovered an Education fund for teachers that had not been used, and took most of the staff to a conference in Nova Scotia, all expenses paid plus a per diem of $100.00 a day. The staff had a great holiday for four days, drinking beer and eating lobster, and showing up for a few lectures. On their return, I was asked if I would care to go to a music conference, and picked the 'Word' conference for choir directors in Vancouver. The Education co-ordinator, Ronnie Michel, gave me a cheque for $1000.00 to cover my flight and expenses. I went to the conference, enjoying the break and returned with new music for the choir, and $400.00, which I had not spent. When I tried to hand the money back, I was told, "Don't be silly, put it in your own account!" There was absolutely no accountability.

Drinking seemed to be a problem on the Reserve, despite being designated a dry Reserve, the booze was smuggled in and of course the teachers and the RCMP had plenty. On the weekends that Bob and I were away, we let some senior grade twelve students clean our house, and in return they were able to wash their hair. Our house was broken into on a regular basis, but after a while, we would leave the door unlocked; we would leave some socks and food for them to take. There was never any vandalism. Most of the parties were at the weekend when I was away, although I did experience a few throughout the year. I had been to one party, which finished up with a few of us in a hot tub, drinking and smoking weed, which was a new experience for me. The following day I fell out the back of a truck, but was not seriously injured.

The teaching year was coming to a close, and I was asked if I would be renewing my contract. I declined because of my family, but otherwise I would have continued, as the past year had been the most satisfying of my teaching career. The final night in Pelican was celebrated with a party for all teachers, school board and some local people. We sat outside sharing the past year with each other and saying our farewells to those who were not returning. There was a police cruiser parked at the back of the school, which was badly vandalized that evening and although we heard sounds of smashing glass, we gave little concern as to anything untoward. As the party came to a close at dawn, I was offered a lift in the same police cruiser back to my lodgings and was asked if I knew anything about the damage. The culprits were never found, even after an extensive investigation lasting two years, involving statements from all the staff. I had my own opinion about what happened that night, but chose to not share it with anyone.

Leaving the following morning, I remember Ronnie Michel with a tear in his eye, giving me a bear hug asking me to reconsider my decision to leave. These Cree Indian people were sensitive, caring, thoughtful, peaceful, and in many ways almost childlike with their gestures. I will never forget them. A music teacher replaced me the following year, but things were never the same; the enthusiasm of the children died and with it the music programme. I kept in touch for the next few years and was pleased to hear that the new school was finally built and students were graduating in bigger numbers.

CHAPTER 35

COME BACK – ALL IS FORGIVEN

I returned to Prince Albert with plans to re-establish my private teaching, and I received a call from Father Cliff Tremblay, who was now the personnel director for the Roman Catholic school board. "Come back, all is forgiven," he said as he explained the programme was in a mess, and Holy Cross had lost its lively spirit when I left. My assignment would be three schools: Holy Cross, St Michael, and St John, all junior high schools. After discussing the offer with my wife, I decided to accept the offer, which would give me more stability than private teaching without benefits. I was to stay for the next six years enjoying my music. I took over the Prince Albert City Band and started to build back the reputation of the band.

The band had reduced in number to only sixteen, with no proper place for practice, and managing with a free classroom in a community college. Equipment and music had to be stored at a private home, the band spending valuable practice time setting up and tearing down for each weekly practice. I managed to build the band back up to over fifty musicians, rehearsing in the basement of the old library, and later the basement of a new town hall. The City of Prince Albert gave us 2,000 square feet of undeveloped basement which, with the help of a loan from the city, managed to build an acoustic band room with attached rooms for an office and a library. Finally we had a proper home, with room for the library and some instruments and music stands. At a later council meeting, the band was forgiven the loan, thanks to the influence of Mayor Dick Spencer.

Prince Albert City Band playing on the riverbank

The band performed on Remembrance Day, Canada Day, and at citizen court gatherings, nursing homes, and seasonal concerts. A marching band was formed for the occasion of the opening of 'Gateway North', a new shopping mall. Prince Albert had a Royal visit from Fergie and Prince Andrew, with the City Band in attendance. It was a scorching hot day in August, as the Royal couple stepped off the plane, making their way towards the band. Before playing the National Anthem, I had the band play 'Let it Snow, let it snow', which we just happened to have in our folders, left over from the Christmas season. The Royal couple appreciated my humour.

The City Band also played for Heritage Days on the river bank in Prince Albert and gave public concerts on an original bandstand, one of two donated by Queen Victoria; the other, so I have been told was placed in the city centre, later torn down and used as a feeding trough at the exhibition grounds. (The Prince Albert City Band is still thriving, and in the capable hands of Robert Gibson, a retired band teacher.)

Later that year the school board hired another band teacher. He had no previous band experience, was ex-RCMP, played the drums, and could speak French, which was how he got hired. These questionable hiring practices were not in the best interest of the student. There was nothing I could do but carry on with my three schools and enjoy my work. Returning home one evening, I received a call from my brother in UK telling me that our mother had been involved in a serious car accident and was in hospital in a coma with little chance of recovering. Once again, Father Cliff Tremblay granted me six weeks leave to visit my mother. I went faithfully, daily to visit her but there was no change in her condition and finally it was agreed that she

My mother with my sister-in-law, Marion

would be taken off the life support machine and given a throat operation, which improved her breathing. Although still in a coma she could understand our conversation and was able to communicate by winking for yes and no to our questions.

My leave came to an end and so I returned to Canada, yet it was only days later when my mother passed away, dying from a massive heart attack. She was eighty-three years old. She had had a good life, and would have had difficulty surviving her multiple injuries, had she lived. I was granted yet another six weeks compassionate leave, with full pay to go home to the UK to bury my mother.

My brother met me at the airport, and we shared a bottle of single malt on the train to Brighton, crying, laughing and remembering our childhood, the war, and the many hilarious happenings involving our mother. We made funeral plans, phoning relatives with the sad news, and placed her house on the market. Our mother had died partly as a result of the car accident, and therefore there had to be an inquest, before we could actually have the funeral. But, after personally driving to the house of the coroner and explaining that I was from Canada, and that time was of the essence, the body was released and our funeral plans went ahead. My brother and I were in the house sorting through her personal effects, trying to remove a wardrobe from her bedroom, but it had become wedged in the doorway. I was on the outer side, and in sheer frustration, I ran to the garage, grabbed an axe and hacked my way through the wardrobe. We both collapsed, laughing, my brother saying: "I bet Mum had a good laugh, watching us."

Clearing a house after death must always be an unpleasant task. It is so final! They are never coming back. Looking under the stairs I found several small hooks, each holding a different length of string. In the war years, everything was useful, and nothing was ever thrown away. Oddly enough, neither of us could find all her jewellery, and only after discussing this with her neighbour, we discovered that the house had been burgled, our mother catching the man in the act. He dropped everything and ran. Since that day our mother had hidden her valuables in good hiding places, so her neighbour told us. We had a pile of things to throw out, including some old shopping bags and cases, which we had placed in the yard for the garbage truck. Today was garbage day, and with the truck just a few houses away, we took it all back inside. After a thorough search, we found the missing, rings, bracelets and other jewellery stuffed down the sides of bags and cases.

The day of the funeral arrived, with Cousin Peggy riding with us in the funeral car. After a few minutes we got the giggles, thinking about some of the antics our mother had been involved in. We really tried to control our mirth, and as we were just one block from the church, still crying with laughter, the funeral director stopped the car and suggested we at least try to look sad. As we turned the final corner, I remember seeing people with heads bowed down, which made it worse, but we were sad nevertheless.

My estranged mother- and father-in-law were at the funeral. They did not speak, but paid their respects. I also saw my daughter, with whom I had not seen or contacted for years; however, after the funeral she joined us in the car and sat on my lap as the hearse drove away. We stopped outside a fish and chip shop on the way to my brother's house, where there was a gathering of my mother's friends. There had been so many humorous times involving my mother, which people remembered and related their story about her. There was the time when my father had invited some important business associates to our house, offering them a glass of sherry, which turned out to be beer in an old sherry bottle. His guests grimaced and did not say a word; instead, they drank the homemade beer. She was the perfect host, generous to everyone, always putting herself last, a wonderful mother and a loving wife to my father. The group of friends chatted, shared photographs of happier times, kissed, hugged, and after several hours went their separate ways. The house sold the following week, and I returned to Canada.

There was some reorganization of schools; St Francis being added to the list. Holy Cross was designated as a French school, but I stayed on as the band teacher, working with teachers who would only speak French, even in the staff room. I found this to be so typically French and rude, when all teachers were fluent in both languages. I decided to play a prank on the staff, writing a phrase in French on the board, asking if someone could help me translate it. I wrote: 'Par d'elle yieux Rhone que nous'. It was absolute rubbish but when said, particularly with a French accent came out as 'Paddle your own canoe'. I had a good laugh, but I don't think the humour was mutual. However, I was always busy, spending little time in the staff room, working with students in the band room at lunch. I have always wondered why some French people are so bloody rude!

I had a confrontation with the personnel director, a new board member, who had scheduled my classes in the three schools, without allowing me the time to travel between them. I was also told that she did not believe in giving spare periods, as preparation was done in the teacher's own time. I found her to be a very cold, insensitive, rude and ignorant with regard to the fine arts, and someone with no experience in the teaching profession, as well as being extremely insecure. Over the next year the situation deteriorated to the point that I was ready to leave, and started looking for an alternative job, and even considered returning to my private teaching. We were coming to the end of 1989 school year, when I received a call from an ex-Principal, who was now the Director of Education for the Rural Division No 56 in Prince Albert. Over the phone he offered me a position teaching at two schools, and asked if I would come down for the interview. And, as one door closed, so another was opened. I was officially given the position and resigned from my current job with the Separate System.

CHAPTER 36

DIVISION 56

My new job was teaching in two schools; Wesmore Junior High, and a rural school in Meath Park, some thirty kilometres out of town. After school I had some private lessons to teach in Prince Albert, and conducting the City Band to keep me busy. Some nights I was working until 20:00 before I returned home, and was beginning to feel the effect of overworking. I continued this for a year, until an unfortunate incident with a student at Meath Park, made my life intolerable. Trying to separate two students who were play fighting with drum sticks after the bell had gone for the last period on a Friday afternoon, I was accused of pushing a student into a pile of music stands. In separating them, I pushed one of them away, perhaps with a little too much force, but without injury. When he arrived home, he informed his parents of the incident—as he saw it—and the next morning I was summoned to the Principal's office, where I was accused of striking a student. These parents were out for blood, and were known for their previous history of causing trouble and verbally attacking teachers.

After a week of listening to their foul language, calling me names, and asking for my resignation, I hired an STF lawyer, who took my complaint, and after much argument, all charges were dropped and the parents withdrew their accusations. I decided to take a few days leave, which would allow me to reflect on the past few months, and what I had been through.

After walking my dog, I went to speak with a friend for his advice. The Reverend Roy Benson—now an Anglican Priest—had been a bandmaster with me in the British Army. We had both emigrated as school band teachers, only he later became a priest. He needed an organist and choirmaster, and offered the paid position to me. If I were to accept, then with permission from the board I could also run my music school from the church basement. I discussed this plan with my wife and accepted his offer, beginning in the fall of that year. I resigned yet again from teaching, this time vowing never to return, or so I thought.

CHAPTER 37

SCHOLFIELD SCHOOL OF MUSIC

I played the organ for all the services at St George's Church, and ran my music school from the church basement during the week. The number of students was growing. I hired four teachers to assist me, including another piano teacher, brass, woodwind and a guitar teacher. Most of the students were involved in conservatory exams and I started theory classes at all levels.

I was working at the band room at the city hall' I had a banging headache and took two tablets to help. I had never used this type of painkiller before, but I discovered later that it had a high dose of codeine. I finished work and went to the Legion and drank some beer with a few friends; getting up from the table, I felt a bit dizzy, but thought nothing of it. One of my friends tried to stop me, but I was belligerent and insisted on driving home. Less than a quarter of a mile's drive back to my home, I passed out and drove into a telegraph pole. When I came round, I started up the engine and drove on, only to be followed by a police car. I was taken to the station, fingerprinted, breathalysed, and found to be over the limit. I could not deny the charge, but I knew that the codeine had made matters worse.

I stood before the judge, who awarded me three months loss of licence, a $600.00 fine or work option, plus attendance at a seminar for drunk drivers. I felt humiliated, embarrassed and wished that I had not driven home that evening. To add to my embarrassment my name was in the local papers for all to see. I now had to walk everywhere, which was a refreshing change although many who felt sorry for me offered lifts. The Reverend Benson had me work at the church as a fine option, practising the organ!

I had played the organ in many different churches throughout my musical career, beginning at Patcham Parish Anglican Church, where I was given some free lessons from a great organist. However, I did not receive any formal training, but worked at using the pedal board and used my piano skills to get through. With the exception of St George's, I gave my service free, and considered my playing as my tithe to the church, receiving payment only for weddings and funerals. Returning home one evening from teaching, I was met by Reverend Benson at my home, where he told me that I had been awarded an Honorary Doctorate of Music from Adam Smith University in Louisiana, U.S.A. Every two years the faculty gave awards to selected people to receive a Doctor of Music, Honorius Causa, and my name had been chosen. I had some business cards made with my new impressive title; Dr. Michael Charles Scholfield. G.R.S.M., B.A (Hons). A (Mus.) L.C.M., Mus. Doc.

There started to be a few conflicts with church activities, and I soon realized that I would have to look for a bigger studio if I was to be successful. There had also been some complaints about me as a Roman Catholic being involved in the Anglican Church, from which I originally came. My drunk driving episode was also not accepted by some of the congregation, or my use of the church as a music school. Finally, after a very successful year at St George's, Reverend Benson politely asked me to leave.

There was a music store in town called Gordie Brandt's, which had adjoining space for a studio. It would be large enough to accommodate the sixty students I already had, and there was room for expansion. I negotiated a lease and secured a bank loan for a grand piano, a Roland Keyboard, an upright piano, a copier, computer, tables, chairs and office furniture. Within the next three months I had just over one hundred students with five teachers on staff. I stopped playing at the church but still kept in touch.

Reverend Benson and I discussed the possibility of staging a performance of Handel's Messiah. The idea appealed to me, and I began planning how to go about this idea. I had decided that there would have to be professional singers for the solo voice parts, an orchestra, and a main chorus body. Before

I could really do anything I would need some money from sponsorship from local business people. I walked into CKBI and ran my idea past Jim Scarrow, who liked my idea and gave me a cheque for $2500.00 to cover payment for the four singers and a professional organist. This was such an encouraging beginning, that I immediately phoned Glen Goodman, an organist from North Battleford, and asked him if he was interested. He accepted the job, and gave me the names of singers who might be able to perform with him.

Within a week I had organized, Gaye-Lyn Kern (soprano), Lisa Hornung (alto), Robert Dick (tenor) and Henri Loiselle (bass). My next task was forming an orchestra, and found that it was not possible to find string players for this, so I would have to improvise. Finally. I came up with an instrumentation of two flutes, two clarinets, oboe, bassoon, trumpet, French horn, Euphonium, tuba and timpani . . . all of whom I recruited from local musicians. I had to rewrite the parts from the main score on my computer. The last task was to encourage singers from all the churches in Prince Albert to form a community choir, to which I had an overwhelming response from many different churches. I then picked four group leaders who could assist me at rehearsals. I acquired enough copies of the music for a large choir, and sent out an invitation to our first get together. Over ninety choir members turned up and sang 'And the Glory of the Lord'. The sound was amazing from such a large group of singers, none of whom were professionals.

We were off to a good start. The following week I handed out a complete rehearsal schedule from January to November, omitting July and August for a summer break. I had rehearsal tapes made for private practice, particularly in the summer months. Each tape had the solo part on one side, and the full choir on the other. I had separate dates for the orchestra to rehearse, plus scheduled practices for the soloists with the organ, and finally selected dates, bringing everything together for one performance at Sacred Heart Cathedral on 22 November, St Cecelia's day, Patron Saint of Music.

Photo from a later performance in Winnipeg

CHAPTER 38

THE MESSIAH

During the course of the next ten months, I encountered a few problems, but nothing that would stop the production. I had to organize risers, printers for the programme, select a venue for a reception following the performance, and organize a scholarships' committee to select recipients for an award. Finally, I had to persuade CBC radio to record this event, by speaking with a director from Montreal, who I embarrassed by telling him that the west of Canada did not get much input from CBC, as most of the good things happened in the east! It was at this point he gave in, and arranged for the entire evening to be recorded.

The evening had arrived. The Oratorio began as the choir assembled, and the orchestra—conducted by Dr. Roy Benson—began the opening overture. The tenor sang

'Comfort Ye My People', followed by 'Every Valley shall be Exulted', and the choir stood and began 'And the Glory of the Lord'.

The evening came to an end and the audience stood in awe after an encore singing the 'Hallelujah' chorus with the choir. Scholarships were awarded, and I was the recipient of the Optimist award for outstanding contribution to music. Later I was interviewed on CKBI and received the outstanding citizen of the month award, presented to me by Jim Scarrow. The entire evening was overwhelming and enjoyable, and afterwards we gathered at reception.

The rent at my studio was reasonable; however, I was struggling financially. To complicate matters, Gordie Brandt's was in financial trouble and planning to declare bankruptcy. After my success with the production of the Messiah, the future now looked grim.

CHAPTER 39

SHERWOOD PARK

I started looking for a teaching position, but did not think I would have any luck as it was already July, and most of the advertised jobs have been filled. There was an advertisement for a band teacher in Sherwood Park, Alberta, which looked promising. I applied for the position and was granted an interview. My only concern was that this position was with the Alliance Church, who would not look too favourably at a Roman Catholic.

I dismissed my fears and arrived for the interview at Strathcona Christian Academy. The building was impressive, excellent landscaping, which was well maintained. As I entered the interview room, twelve people—mostly church members—sat at a table. I was introduced by the superintendent, and was asked to tell them about myself. I was succinct, honest and tried to create the impression that I really needed this job. I was asked many questions, some from Connie Mycroft who was the Principal, and some from church school board members. One odd question was asked about what I thought about homosexuality, to which I replied: "Surely you don't condone it, do you?" I believe this question was removed from the interview list! I already held a teaching certificate from Saskatchewan, and was told I would be granted a certificate to teach in Alberta. I think the board were impressed with my Mus. Doc, honorary, my experience as a conductor and teaching record. Before being offered the position, the board wanted to meet my wife, Rosemary, who passed the interview charming everyone. I was offered the position and would start in September.

I moved to Sherwood Park, leaving Rosemary in Prince Albert to fulfil her contract with the Separate School Board. After meeting with the superintendent, I was taken to meet a church family, where I could lodge until I was settled. They were very kind, and treated me as one of the family. There were no children, except a grown-up son, who lived elsewhere but would turn up to see his parents when he needed help.

Prayers were said before each meal, sometimes a reading from the bible, and later a discussion about its meaning. Frankly, I thought this was a little over the top, but the husband was the one in control in this family, his submissive wife following along in silence. I got to know them well, and was grateful for their help and hospitality.

The following week I was introduced to the staff at the Academy. A curious collection of mainly younger teachers, all treading very carefully, especially about what you said. Each morning there was prayer before school, which was actually quite enjoyable. We would sing a few songs, and then one teacher would lead the session with a reading, followed by a meditation. Each teacher would take a turn at presenting a theme; I was dreading the thought of what I would do when my turn came, but that was a long way off yet. The church, made employees sign an agreement stating that they could not smoke, drink, along with a number of other pleasantries. It would seem that the church did your thinking for you and took ten percent of your salary after you had given them your T4. Most teachers followed this rule, although I was never sure whether it was mandatory. It appeared that most teachers were brain washed, scared to express any real personal thoughts, and encouraged to report any different behaviour to a higher echelon. Teachers were always looking over their shoulder, and often I found groups of them gathered in corners discussing something private. The powers that be were going to find me a tough one to break!

My financial situation had worsened yet again, coping with paying for two rented houses—one in Prince Albert and the other in Sherwood Park. My car was repossessed, and I replaced it with an old Grande Marquis, which my friends named HMS Pinafore. I was advised to declare bankruptcy for a second time, which turned out to be poor advice. This course of action could have been avoided, had I not acted so quickly. It seemed that my life had been a continual struggle handling money and, as I grew older, there were no signs of improvement.

Bringing two families together, moving from place to place and never really settling, could have contributed to my financial situation. I have often asked myself whether coming to Canada was the right decision and have tried on each visit back to the UK, to lay my ghost without success. That was until my last visit in 2014.

Our four sons, Simon, Clive, Malcolm and Alex

Our four daughters; back row, Emma and
Julia. Front row; Sarah and Amanda

Rosemary, Melissa, Charles, Emma, and myself – 2011

Melissa, Grandpa and Emma

At Sherwood Park—and the frustration of certification at Strathcona Christian Academy—it soon became clear that my credentials were insufficient to be given an Alberta teaching certificate, but I could remain teaching under the licence of the Principal. Application was made, and a letter sent to the Minister of Education, asking him to review my case, but this was denied. I enjoyed my classes, and although the standard of playing was below average, I could work on that for improvement. To make my workload full time, I taught a group of thirteen failed English students, and a full class for Career and Life Management; both classes were fun to teach, particularly the English group, who responded to my teaching. At a staff meeting, we were asked to form a group of four, given a basic receipt, and produce a breakfast meal the following day. I had already made friends with two rebels, who picked our fourth person. We met that night at a house and planned our meal for the following day. I took a bottle of wine along to liven up the evening, and to see their reaction. Despite the rules, we all had a glass, and added the remainder of the bottle into our breakfast quiche. The following day, with our quiche demolished, we were asked "what was the secret to the delicious taste". Naturally, we did not divulge our secret ingredient, or we could have lost our jobs.

I went to my first Sunday church service at the Alliance Church, which consisted of a show, with a big stage band, playing jazzed up arrangements of (so called) sacred music. A scripture reading and prayers followed this, and then we were treated to a country and western style song, sung by some yahoo, complete with cowboy boots, hat and jeans. I almost burst out laughing, but made it in time to the washroom, returning with a dignified look on my face, just in time for communion, which consisted of a biscuit and some cherry aid. As a Catholic, I was just not expecting this, and later mentioned the time when Jesus turned the water into wine, to which I was informed, "Ah, but the wine was not fermented." Now I was convinced that the entire congregation were brainwashed. I felt as though I had not been to church, and went to a Catholic church for a later service. *What have I got myself into?* I thought, but was determined to see this year through. My wife would be joining me shortly, and we would be moving into our rented home on Cedar Street.

I returned to Prince Albert, loaded up our household effects, and drove to Sherwood Park; my wife would be arriving at the end of the month. It was late when I arrived, and was anxious to empty the U-Haul. Working on my own, I fell on the stairs whilst moving a fridge. I felt bruised, but could still function.

Finally, my wife joined me and we both settled in our new rented house. As the weeks passed by, my shoulder was becoming dysfunctional, and later it was confirmed by a doctor that I had torn the rotator cuff in my left shoulder. The waiting list in Alberta for surgery was long, and I was prescribed a narcotic (Percocet), which I took daily and continued teaching in a semi daze, smiling my way through the course of each day. Because of my condition, my teacher evaluation was postponed, until a more convenient time. I managed to get a place for surgery in Saskatchewan, which would be much sooner for me than my wait in Alberta.

After surgery I returned to Sherwood Park, but could not resume teaching for another month. My employers were not happy, and not only hired a substitute teacher, but replaced me while I was sick. After several interviews with the Superintendent, it became clear that I was not wanted; someone had been bad mouthing me in my absence, questioning my moral standards. I was uncertain as to what action I was going to take, but for safety, I hired a lawyer. On my last day, I received my final pay cheque, and was asked to sign a form declaring that I could not take legal action against the school. I phoned my lawyer, who told me to sign it, as the form was meaningless. This was followed by months of wrangling, and unpleasant accusations from the Academy. This entire case was going to be resolved at a meeting which, if not acceptable, would be decided in a courtroom. Having found yet another rented house back in Prince Albert, I had made plans to leave Sherwood Park in order to set up my private teaching practice to survive. Along with the Superintendent, parents and students came to help us pack up the removal truck, which was much appreciated. I had my arm in a sling, and Rosemary had slipped and broken a bone in her foot; I was driving a big U-Haul with one arm, and my wife following behind, driving with her left foot in a cast. We did, however, receive some strange looks as we limped and staggered towards the gas pumps to refuel our vehicles.

CHAPTER 40

RETURNING TO PRINCE ALBERT

Arriving back in Prince Albert, we quickly settled into our rented accommodation, where there was plenty of room for me to teach. I also took a teaching post at a local music academy, teaching Technics piano. I received a phone call from the Superintendent, who wanted to put things right and come to some compromise without the need to take the matter to court. I agreed. I told him that all I wanted was some compensation to cover my move back to Saskatchewan. We agreed on a figure, and the case was closed. God works in mysterious ways, and I believe that he is in charge, and not us!

The following Monday morning I was replacing a light above the front porch, when I fell and smashed my right shoulder. It was confirmed at the hospital that I had now torn the rotator cuff on my right shoulder. I arranged for surgery, got the same surgeon, who remarked that I would qualify for "frequent rotator cuff points".

While recovering in hospital I received a letter from the British Government who, because of my shoulder injury and being unable to work, were granting me my Army pension earlier than expected. I could not believe my luck, and the timing of receiving cash when I really needed it.

I had known Dr. David Stevens for some time, first meeting him when I went to teach his two sons play the piano. Chatting with him one evening, we discovered that he had worked in Brighton where I grew up. Further discussion revealed that his sons and I had lessons from the same teacher, a Miss Muriel Hart. I had my first lesson in 1947, and she was still teaching. I also discovered that David had worked at the Brighton General, where my mother was taken after the car crash. Dr. Stevens had operated on my mother, making a hole in her throat to enable her to speak.

Job cuts at the hospital were coming, and nurses did not know who was on the list. Morale was poor, and David asked me if I would go along with a prank to cheer everyone up. The plan was to act like I was suffering from deafness, and I was to receive an implant for my left ear, while causing as much disruption as possible. My name was Dr. Konk, a Jehovah Witness, and extremely deaf. The only person who was to know about this was the hospital administrator. I exchanged my clothes for a hospital gown and as I lay on the bed I started causing trouble. A nurse asked me if I had been to the bathroom, to which I replied: "I parked my motor bike in the car park." The nurse repeated, louder each time, until finally giving up.

Dr. Stevens said to the nurses, "Don't take any notice of that old bastard, he's as deaf as a post."

I responded by saying: "I heard what you said, you're a bozo, and shouldn't speak to patients like that." The nurses began defending the Doctor and while they apologized for him, I leapt out of bed—gown wide open—and ran down the nearest corridor. I had chosen a dead end, and turned to face the music. The game was up, and I had to admit my part in the prank. The nurses had a good laugh, and I had made their Friday afternoon, one to remember and smile about. The staff nurse looked at me and with a smile said, "Don't ever get sick." It was at this hospital that I had my second rotator cuff surgery, and while waiting to have the operation, a nurse whispered in my ear, "How's your hearing?"

CHAPTER 41

RETURN TO PRIVATE TEACHING

I set up some private teaching at a school in Christopher Lake, some forty kilometres from Prince Albert, and had sufficient number of students to drive out two days a week. I was also asked to help the Separate School Board set up its defunct band programme, which involved finding instruments, assessing their value and making a report with recommendations.

I had two sons living in Winnipeg; Malcolm was working as a translator (self-employed), and Alex was working for an envelope company. Alex's wife Kim, was a Pharmacist for Shopper's Drugmart. Rosemary and I drove to Winnipeg to celebrate my sixtieth birthday, spending several days visiting and enjoying the city. On our return journey, we started thinking about considering a move to Winnipeg. Further discussion as we travelled, revealed that it would be a good move for us.

There were grandchildren to visit, and Winnipeg had a good music reputation for all styles, plus I had already been asked if I was interested in conducting Northwinds Community Band.

CHAPTER 42

MOVING TO WINNIPEG

Arriving back home, we started to pack up. We planned to leave a year later so I pre-paid the removals, handed over my students to another teacher, and secured yet another rental house in Winnipeg. On 1 July we made the long journey to Winnipeg; Alex drove the truck, while I acted as co-pilot. The house was small. It had half a basement (which was damp), but it was close to downtown and seemed to be in a nice location, which our younger son had chosen. Another good reason for moving was the news that Alex and Kim were expecting a baby. Malcolm and Sandy had two children: Maia and Nicholas.

The following week I was asked if I was interested in conducting the Northwinds Community Band. I turned up on a Wednesday evening, conducted a few pieces and accepted the offer. This band had a great spirit, and welcomed me as their conductor. I have many pleasant memories of my time with this group, as it grew in numbers and musical proficiency. I spent twelve years with them and I believe was the longest serving director of this band. A month later I was playing Tuba in Westwood Community Band, and although not a trained tuba player, I was able to help out in that section. The conductor was Tony Klein—a tuba player—who became a good friend. He resigned that year, and I was asked to take over. Within the year, I was running two community bands, and had set up ten private piano lessons from my home.

Alex had located Christ the King Catholic Church on St Mary's Road, which we tried the following Sunday. We sat waiting for the service to begin, but there was a problem with the priest, who had got his dates mixed up, and thought another priest was covering the mass that Sunday. After, some frantic phone calls, order was restored with an apologetic priest rushing to the church. We tried another church the following Sunday, which was nearer to our home, but we could not understand the priest from Vietnam, who was struggling with his English. We returned the following Sunday to Christ the King and, discovering that there was no organist, I played for the song leader, Lynda, with whom I shared my music for the next thirteen years.

I decided to put on another production of the 'Messiah' at Christ the King. I had the music already scored for a group and would need to buy enough choral books for the choir. My plan would be different from my previous production in Prince Albert. I made up a letter inviting choirs to join our chorus, sending it to as many churches in Winnipeg, regardless of the denomination. I approached the Canadian Choral Federation for advice on purchasing choral parts, and they donated fifty books. I found a competent organist, Nancy Nowosad, who agreed to play for us; however, finding soloist singers was going to be a challenge. I got permission to use the church, and formed a group of willing helpers to take some of the tasks in setting the stage. I had someone draw up a seating plan, organize risers, start a phoning plan, and press coverage. Olga Novak was the treasurer, keeping a count of tickets sold and asking for donations from sponsors. We were going to award scholarships for young students entering university in the field of fine arts. I was conducting two community bands, and was able to find musicians. Rehearsals were on Sunday afternoons, splitting into four groups, and later coming together with organ accompaniment. To be able to stage this performance, we had to remove the altar and move several pews around. During this time, services were held in the basement, thanks to the cooperation of Father Renato Pasinato, who was the local priest. After months of hard work at rehearsals, and with singers from twelve local churches in Winnipeg, the performance proved to be a great success,

I was asked to adjudicate school bands across Canada, in Saskatoon, The Pas, Edmonton, Calgary, Rainy River, Fort McMurray, Yellowknife, Sudbury, Ottawa, and Toronto. I returned to Ottawa four times to grade the bands from that area. One of the bands was from Quebec and outplayed all the other bands each year, setting high standards for everyone.

These students were from Grade 5/6, playing at a Grade 9 level, observing all the dynamics, producing a good sound and very disciplined. I had a CD made of their performance and played the music to my community bands in Winnipeg, who thought they were listening to a senior band.

CHAPTER 43

RRVJA AND CHRIST THE KING

In 2002, there was an advertisement looking for help with a new band programme at Red River Valley Junior Academy in Winnipeg. This was a Seventh Day Adventist private school, and I was hesitant to go for the interview. Speaking with the Principal, Mr. Mighty, I soon felt at ease and asked him what he needed. There had been a band programme ten years prior to this, and parents were asking for the band to start again. I proposed a two-day workshop for the students, which would give them an idea of what to expect. I hired a friend, Ozzy Aasland, to assist me with the workshop. After renting the instruments from Long & McQuade, we introduced a band programme to twenty interested students, which was an instant success. It seemed that the Principal had assumed that I would be teaching this course, and I had no intention of becoming a teacher again, attending meetings, signing a contract . . . no thanks, those days were gone. However, under my terms I would consider the position, which were very different. No contract or meetings, work only mornings after 09:00 and finish by midday. Payment was to be made monthly by personal cheque. Mr. Mighty said to me, "I have no problem with that. When can you start?"

Working with well-disciplined students was a challenge but highly rewarding. The classes at Red River were smaller and we had an excellent budget to work with. I was able to buy what was needed, without question, and was never refused any request. I found the staff, pleasant, helpful, supportive and flexible. When a conflict arose, the staff would switch days to accommodate my plans, something I have never been able to do in the other school systems. Grouping of students was different at this school, and because of the small size, grades were joined together; grades 1 to 2, 3 to 4 and through to 9 to 10. I am not sure that I agree with this system, but I did not hear any complaints. The band was originally started in grade 7, which I moved down to grade 6. The students had some music instruction prior to joining the band, which was not an elective, but the entire grade participated. Testing a grade 6 student for placement on an instrument one day, I asked how she had enjoyed the recorder that year. Her response was: "You have no idea how brutal it was!" I found the only problem with smaller children taking band was that there were not too many that could take the trombone, simply because of size.

Each year there was a trip to Bismarck, North Dakota, USA, at the Dakota Adventist Academy, some thirteen kilometres from the city. This was a large complex of over 4,000 square feet, which had been full of students in earlier years. Student population in recent years has been on the decline, mainly because of cost to the parents.

On my first visit to DAA, the students joined other small private schools from near locations, forming a large choir of one hundred students and band at two levels. Art, photography, hand bells, strings and guitar were also offered. The Academy had its own school bus, which would arrive in Winnipeg to pick our group of thirty-five students with chaperones, deliver them to DAA, and return after the four-day music festival. There was no band programme at the Academy the first year, but after our inspiring concert, a small band was formed from the Grade10–12 students.

The band programme was growing at RRVJA, with numbers of over seventy students keen for instruction. And to help me, I hired an assistant, Ozzy Aasland, a colleague from Westwood Community Band. He was a talented musician, ex-Canadian Air Force Command Band, had a great sense of humour, and was respected by the students. Each trip to Bismarck, I would accompany Ozzy in his old van, equipped with snow tires and make the long trip. We opted to stay in a hotel, and travel to the Academy daily, rather than stay with the students. The accommodation was rustic in style, very warm, and cockroaches were in the rooms. The premises needed major renovation, with the roof leaking, mould in the rooms and renewal of the furnace and boiler systems. In the later years, these problems were addressed, after the school received some hefty donations; but I am not sure about the cockroaches!

Another reason for our not staying at the Academy was the menu. According to the official Seventh Day Adventist Dietetic website, SDAs have been vegetarians for over a century. No meats were allowed in their diets, including beef, chicken, fish and wild game. Eggs and dairy were acceptable, and legumes and beans, but only in moderation. With this kind of diet everyone was continually farting at band practice, which, given the unpleasant aroma, was really hard to take. Now perhaps, dear reader, you can appreciate the wisdom of booking a hotel, where Ozzy and I could indulge in a steak and a good glass of red wine. The SDAs believed that after alcohol and tobacco—both of which were banned—meat was the next worse item you could put in your body. However, I must say that we were always cordially welcomed and treated with respect and kindness by the staff at the Academy.

Our staff consisted of just ten teachers: the Principal Ian Mighty, Mr. Prime, Dan McGuire, Lana Landry, Mr. and Mrs. Gordon, Ms. Dawes, Ms. Sampson, and Ozzy Aasland and myself, all of whom were guided by our wonderful school secretary, Lora Toop, who was always so helpful with every situation; *thank you, Lora for making my stay at RRVJA a happy one.* Apart from myself, there were two other rebels on the staff who kept us on our toes. Mr. Prime, in his eighties, teaching physical education, would often pull me aside to share a joke in the hallway, and is best remembered for his Christmas cake, laced with Jamaican rum! Dan McGuire was assistant Principal, and taught a Grade 5/6 class, which was situated across from my band room, where I could hear his antics with his class; we would both shout back and forth teasing our students. One year, Dan introduced me to a new teacher, as the Superintendent of the Adventist Schools; however, our joke did not last long, as I could not contain my laughter. Dan bought a motorbike and one day he arrived at school to show off his latest prize to all the students. However, there was an occasion when the Principal was away at a conference, so with a student riding pillion, Dan roared up down the main corridor of the school, much to the amusement of the pupils. *Dan, you are one in a million!*

My band room was moved to various rooms over the years, originally placed next to the main office. The Principal held an evening meeting in the Band room, moving several stands and chairs, having his meeting and leaving the room without tidying up after. When I arrived the following morning, I asked the secretary what had happened in the band room. My response was to place a table across the desk in the Principal's office, and wait to see his reaction; he laughed and said to me, "I get the message, Dr. Scholfield." Ian Mighty ran a happy school, and established a good spirit amongst the students.

Whilst I was teaching at RRVJA, Christ the King Catholic School, K-8 approached me with a view to begin a band programme, starting in grade 7. It would most certainly be an added plus for the school, and would be the first of its kind in the area. I discussed the idea with Ozzy, and we both agreed we could manage one day a week for this project. I set up interviews for instrument choices, and in September of that year, the programme kicked off. Ozzy aged eighty, and myself at seventy-one years old, were going to attempt to teach students from Grade 7 and 8, which we knew could be challenging. We would arrive before school and set up the room, encouraging students to come in early for a practice before lessons had begun. Initially we had a good response, but attendance dwindled after the novelty wore off. Most of the students did not practice, and the sound from full band was quite brutal. Occasionally, there was part of a tune that was recognizable, however, only when the drums were resting.

Within the first three months I had some of the students actually playing in church without scaring the congregation away, and later the full band entertained an audience before the Christmas Nativity play. Despite the lack of musical ability, our students showed good spirit trying their best, and enjoying the class, which was only once in a six-day cycle and not enough time to produce anything of merit. With a shared facility used as a library and an actual music room for general music, it was quite a struggle.

Our band class was scheduled on the only day that this classroom was free. It was used for music for the lower grades, taught by Josephine Mots, who had the task of teaching large numbers of students—some of whom were reluctant—to stage a Christmas musical each year. Josephine worked many hours over and above her normal time, working through lunchtime to rehearse the choir. "They don't deserve you!" With the band programme there was a measure of success, but having to set up and tear down the room each practice was not encouraging. In addition, the attitude of the majority of students who did not practice, along with the standard of musical prowess, was non-existent, despite there being an attempt by some to produce a better sound. I arranged a band workshop at the school, adding my students from RRVJA to play with the new students. This was a lot of fun, and everyone learnt something that day, finishing with a mini concert to the parents. Both Ozzy and I were finding the workload to be too much, and resigned the following year, handing over the task to Suzanna Libby, a teacher and a colleague from a community band.

I have many pleasant memories from my teaching days, both at DAA and RRVJA, which I believe are still operating with success. In 2013, at the age of seventy-three, I had made the decision to finally resign. Ozzy, who was eighty-two, decided to hang up his hat too. At our farewell concert, I invited my community band to play with the school bands, finishing the evening with massed band performance of 'Stand up, Stand up for Jesus'. Later that week, both Ozzy and I were invited to a farewell dinner, at which I was asked to make a speech. I had nothing prepared, and always believe it better to be spontaneous, which can be dangerous! I recall that I was feeling on the dangerous side that night and revealed an occurrence that had happened in the classroom the previous year. I was playing the piano to demonstrate how a new band piece would sound. My faithful assistant Ozzy was turning pages for me, when suddenly the whole manuscript fell to the floor. Ozzy audibly responded with *fuck!* Silence followed until a Grade 9 student said, "Don't worry, Mr. Aasland, we won't tell." The look on the faces of the staff, Principal and a pastor, was priceless, but they laughed heartily at my story. I miss my relationship with these people, for they were the best people I had ever worked with in my teaching career. *Good luck, and God bless all of you!*

CHAPTER 44

CADETS

I became involved with a Cadet corps, working as a band instructor for a small group. Due to the absence of one of the teachers, I accompanied the group to a band workshop and was asked to step in to instruct. I began working on the music for a parade with the cadets, with the standard of playing graded as pretty awful. The main issue was the intonation, plus there were varying standards of musicianship and experience within the group. Rehearsing the National Anthem (the Queen), I stopped the band, and asked the tuba players to play what they had, as something was not right. I discovered that whoever had arranged this score, had given the melody to the basses! I laughed, saying, "What musical moron wrote this I wonder," just as the director of the camp walked in the room. Later I found out that it was his arrangement.

That following summer I was invited as a civilian instructor to work in Penhold AB. I would be working for eight weeks with other instructors, teaching cadets, conducting bands, and working with them on parade. I arrived at the camp on a hot summer's day, just in time for supper at 17:00, only to be told that I was not allowed in the dining hall without socks with my sandals. I could see that this was going to be an interesting eight weeks. Later that day, I had to fill out forms, giving my personal information for payroll purposes, asking for my social insurance number in five different places. I had served over sixteen years in the British Army, and had forgotten the 'bullshit'. The other instructors were younger than me, some in their fourth year at university, and others were teachers from bands across Canada. We worked well together, sharing our experiences, and learning from one another. We all spent time in the mess, enjoying a crazy game at the billiard table, the name of which escapes me, however, it involved sliding the balls across the table at high speed to eliminate your opponent's. There could have been as many as ten or more people playing this exhausting game. According to ability the recruits formed several bands, who spent six weeks at the camp in summer, enjoying the music and band engagements, marching band and concerts.

These cadet camps attracted young boy and girl cadets from across Canada, spending six weeks of musical instruction from qualified instructors who were in their third year at university studying music training to become a band teacher in a school. The music section was just a small part of the many cadets who attended this course. It was at Penhold that I first met Kara Martens, who was from Windsor, and would be teaching in my section. Kara was a brass instructor, but had string experience playing the viola; I told her that I was a poor second violin player, with my main instrument being the bassoon. Several years later, I moved to Winnipeg where Kara had moved, and we both were involved with a new string quartet, called the 'Cathedral Avenue', which was the name of the street where she lived.

One of the civilian instructors was a young man named Andrew, who played in a Salvation Army band from Ontario. Several of us were drinking in the mess, enjoying draught Guinness on tap, which Andrew thought he might try for his first drink. After downing almost half in one swallow, he placed the glass down and remarked: "Nectar of the Gods," with a big smile on his face. It was at Penhold that I met John Martens from Winnipeg, Kara from Windsor, and Celine from Calgary, whose friend Caroline would sing menus in restaurants. Working with these people was an experience I am glad to have had, learning from each other and having fun. We all became good friends during the eight weeks, enjoying each other's company, and playing music every day. John Martens married Kara and they both went on to teach band at Winnipeg school division.

CHAPTER 45

SUMMERLAND AND DUDLEY

Our home in Winnipeg turned out to be very damp, and so I started to look for another house. I came across a large apartment near the university, which was on the fourteenth floor and in good condition. I often wondered if we would ever settle and have a home of our own again, which seemed unlikely at that time. Our new apartment was part of a huge complex of 400 suites. It was designed exclusively for senior adults and divided by an enclosed atrium, where the indoor temperature was constant and comfortable all year round, and the only one of its kind in Winnipeg. The plants were lush and green and the atmosphere was serene, all enhanced by a year-round heated pool. *Oh, I almost forgot to mention the owner, who was a God-fearing, money grabbing devout Christian.* Despite all that the complex was full of students, who partied most nights, while other inappropriate activities took place. We stayed for three years, trying to ignore the parties and noise from the Atrium that echoed and could be heard by all the residents who had inside apartments.

Alex and Kim found a house for us on Dudley Avenue, and after making an offer, we moved into our new home in March. Two years later, Clive, Alex and some friends, built a garage and landscaped the back yard. The kitchen and bathroom were remodelled, and we replaced the windows and had a new furnace with air conditioning installed. The house was only 680 square feet, and the basement—although finished—had a low ceiling and needed some upgrading, but was big enough for our master bedroom, as the rooms upstairs were too small. The neighbourhood was a good area, close to shopping malls, church and schools, and we had bought the house at the right time, with house prices rising significantly after we had purchased.

CHAPTER 46

CATHEDRAL AVENUE STRING QUARTET

After settling in Winnipeg, I made contact with Kara Martens, who in conversation with me earlier, had mentioned that she had played the viola and if I ever moved to Winnipeg, we should get together and attempt to form a string quartet. Kara had a friend that not only played the violin, but also was friendly with a cellist. We arranged to meet in a shopping mall at Christmas time and play a few carols for the shoppers. It was a great success, and after two hours of playing, we had two enquiries asking if we could play at weddings that summer.

My first choice has always been classical music, which I find satisfying, challenging, enjoyable and never boring. My newfound companions were of the same thoughts, none of us were playing at a professional level, competent enough to tackle the demands of string quartet literature. We worked on a Mozart work for several months, with some success, although it was not easy finding the time or discipline to practice. Our first cellist was Eric, a mature student studying for a PhD in physics, and Kara, our viola player was a band teacher in Winnipeg. Christine our first violinist was a lawyer, and myself a band teacher at a private school. We all had a common interest, which was a passion for playing, giving us a lot of fun, rehearsing and performing. Our cellist, Eric was our MC, announcing our programme to our audience, and always did a superb job. On one occasion we were to play a work by Cesar Franck, which was announced as 'Penis Angelicus' instead of 'PANIS Angelicus'. For future performances, we discarded this piece from our repertoire.

We met to rehearse in the homes of Christine and Kara; both these homes had a place for us to practice. Sitting on a shelf and watching our rehearsal was a cat, waiting to pounce on Christine during the piece. I would find myself looking away from my music and at the cat, wondering when he would make his move. Arriving at Kara's home, we would be greeted by loud barking of their two dogs, Sam and Ella, correctly pronounced as 'Salmonella'. Ella was a rescue dog and would retreat to the top of the stairs as we entered, but over a period of time, slowly descended step by step, until finally coming to us and eventually allowing us to pet her.

The quartet was hired to play at a wedding, held outside by a riverbank on a hot summer's day, battling the black fly that were attacking us. The preacher was long winded, and it seemed that he would never stop, at which time I leant over the music stand by Kara and wrote: "Shut up and fuck off!" To this day, Kara tells me that my pencilled comment remains on her music. Terrence, a retired editor of the Winnipeg Free Press (who filled the position with competence and was always the perfect gentleman, and had a great sense of humour), replaced our cellist. I miss my association with this group and will never forget the fun I had with them.

CHAPTER 47

LAST YEARS IN WINNIPEG

I returned to working with cadets at Cold Lake, acting as a Director of the Service Band, spending eight weeks in the summer teaching music. The summer camp was normally held in a high school but was unavailable, so the alternative was hanger 8, which was not in use, except for an emergency situation. We had to go through security, sign in and out each day, which we thought a bit pointless. However, looking at the sign in and out book one evening, I discovered that Andrew Wahl, another civilian instructor, had been writing some amusing names in the book. Mickey Mouse, the Lone Ranger, but the best one was Iva Stiffy, which must have brought a smile to people's faces. Andrew was a competent clarinet player, and great fun to work with, and definitely "off the wall". I was introduced to the resident band at Cold Lake, consisting of volunteers from the base. I was invited to play tuba on their practice night. So I would walk in, grab a beer, and then sit down and play.

Now, this was more like it; what a great way to rehearse! I was not a good tuba player but enjoyed the challenge and could sight-read the music on a gig. I was invited to join a German 'Oomph' group playing to celebrate a fiftieth anniversary. Dressed in borrowed lederhosen, we were taken to the back garden of a home where we were playing. We set up and began playing for a large group of over one hundred guests, who were enjoying the celebration. One of the guests offered the band a glass of raspberry schnapps, which turned out to be moonshine. After sniffing mine, I decided not to try the unknown drink, which was a good decision; however the trombone player had two glasses and landed up asleep in the vegetable plot. We finished and returned to the camp and were dropped off by our billets.

I slept well and got up early ready to play at church that morning. As I left my block I noticed the van that had taken me to the party; it was parked on the road where I had found two of the band members who had spent the night sleeping in the van as they could not remember where their quarters were. *So much for moonshine!* Working with cadets is very rewarding, but you need lots of energy, working long days, and beginning with an early 06:00 workout. I made a decision to make this my last appearance with the cadet corps, as my knees were giving out on climbing stairs and I wanted to explore other musical ideas.

Members of the Messiah Choir had asked me to stage another performance at Christ the King. We began contacting everyone, and had to look at finding new soloist singers. But within the month we had everything in place, including the same organist, Nancy, and four new faces for the soloist parts: Tracy Vestby, Julian Vanderput, John Parry and Barry Schmidt. Our youngest singer and soloist was ten-year-old Amy Vaillancourt, who had a music résumé that would be impressive for a singer twice her age. A trilingual singer, she performed in two French choirs and sang in the Tagalog language at the Philippine Pavilion at Folklorama. As her birthday fell on the night of the performance, it turned out to be a very special night for her. The performance raised funds for scholarships in Fine Arts at Manitoba universities.

My youngest son Alex treated me to a trip to England for my seventieth birthday, which included a visit to see Liverpool play Wigan at Anfield. I placed a ten-pound bet to forecast the score: Liverpool 2 – Wigan 1, and received seventy pounds back. I also got to go to the new Arsenal stadium, which held 60,000 people, and saw Arsenal beat Hull 3-0. We stayed two nights at the Hard Day's Night Hotel, in the John Lennon Suite, priced at £600.00 per night. We got a reduced price to £400.00. (Prices now in 2015 are £1250.00 per night, which has doubled in five years!) The suite included a baby grand piano (supposedly used by John Lennon), complimentary fully stocked bar, slippers and fresh flowers. My birthday treat continued with a visit to the Royal Albert Hall in London, for a performance of the Messiah, to celebrate its 250th anniversary.

My seventieth celebration was unforgettable, returning back to Canada just ahead of a snowstorm in England. *Thank you, Alex, for a memorable seventieth birthday. I can't wait for my eightieth!*

Alex took us to Hawaii over the Christmas break, staying in Honolulu at a big hotel. Alex had also arranged for Simon, Celine, Christopher and Spencer to travel from Shanghai to celebrate the season with us. Rosemary was unaware of the plan, and while neither one of us had seen the children, keeping this a secret before December was going to be tricky. Settling in at the hotel, the youngest grandchild Spencer knocked at our door; we made sure Rosemary opened the door and, having never seen her youngest grandchild, thought there had been an error until the rest of the family appeared. What a wonderful Christmas gift this was, as we spent the next ten days with them.

CHAPTER 48

UK VISIT

The following summer my wife and I, Emma and grand-daughter Melissa went to Wales to visit Rosemary's father, who was ninety-one years old. We booked our flights with Iceland Express, a budget flight from Winnipeg to Iceland, and then to Gatwick. The flight was a nightmare, from boarding to deplaning. Only minutes before take-off the seat beside me was still vacant when at the very last moment, a harried looking man clutching a well-worn bag and sweating profusely, looked in my direction as the stewardess pointed him to the last remaining seat. He stuffed his bag in the overhead bin and slumped down beside me. "Nearly bloody missed it," he snorted as he wiped the sweat from his face and fidgeted with his seat belt. I could smell booze as he leaned towards me, pushing his knees into the seat in front, causing the woman in the seat to turn round and glare at him. "Sorry, Ma'am, just trying to fit in," he said with a grin. I turned and looked out of the window trying to ignore him, thinking it was just my luck to have a drunk sit next to me, when I noticed what looked like our suitcases on a stationary trolley as we began to taxi towards the runway.

The seats were really small, and I too had difficulty fitting my knees into the small space, finally turning them at an angle. Eating was going to be difficult as the tray would not lie flat to place anything on safely. Headsets were being handed out for the feature film. My daughter bought some only to discover that the main feature was in Icelandic with no subtitles. We all had a good chuckle and my spirits lifted thinking about our trip to England, spending time with my father-in-law in Wales. My granddaughter would be seeing her great-grandfather for the first time in her life. I had a good feeling about this holiday and was looking forward to the flight.

How wrong I was. The pest next to me began ordering double gin and tonics, whilst complaining about the seating and the absence of ice for his drink. "What sort of Mickey Mouse airline is this anyway," he blurted to several passengers, who by now were looking at him. The stewardess looked at me, rolled her eyes, and then smiled at the friendly drunk as she gave him his fifth gin. The seats were uncomfortable, and having two total knee replacements, I found that I could no longer remain seated in the same position for any longer. I had no option but to get up and walk towards the back of the plane. "Another gin and tonic," I heard the pest yell out to the stewardess as she disappeared through the curtain, and in an even louder voice added, "and find some bloody ice!" I got chatting with a young couple that also mentioned they had seen what looked like their suitcases on a trolley as the plane departed. The film finished and passengers were told to fasten seat belts due to rough weather ahead. I got back to my seat, hoping that the friendly drunk was asleep, but as I sat down he ordered another gin. I was entertained for the remainder of the flight with him telling me and the rest of the passengers how he was going to write a letter of complaint about this Mickey Mouse airline; his main concern was that there was no ice for his gin.

Finally, we arrived in Reykjavik, Iceland. There would be a short break whilst passengers lined up to get boarding passes for the flight to Gatwick. I could not believe what I saw – angry, frustrated passengers complaining about the delay as they waited while the airport staff made out boarding passes with a pen! Apparently the computers were not functioning, and each pass was handwritten, taking far too much time. The plane would be leaving late, and passengers with connections at Gatwick, would miss their scheduled flight. Our friendly drunk was right about the poor service, as all the shops were closed and the only place open were the toilets. Eventually we went through security only to discover that there were two more checks. I began to wonder if in fact there was an alert of some sort, but nobody seemed to know anything.

Boarding the plane I discovered that our seating plan had been changed, and our friendly drunk got to entertain another group of passengers. Most of us were tired, including the drunk (I think the steward cut him off the gin!). Seated now in the first four rows, I turned and noticed that passengers were sleeping, so I closed my eyes too. We awoke to an announcement that we would be landing in the next twenty minutes, and as the plane came to a halt, we gathered our hand luggage, everyone thankful that the plane had made it safely and our uncomfortable flight was over. However, the airline had yet another surprise in store for everyone.

The real nightmare was just about to begin. We stood gazing hopefully at the empty carousel, wishing our luggage to appear, but not one case could be seen. The airline had managed to misplace the luggage for the entire plane. We were all very angry, however, with the promise that we would receive our luggage the following day, the only alternative was to fill out a form for lost luggage.

What a fiasco; our luggage finally arrived eight days later, delivered to the house late at night. We did later receive some compensation from the airline of one hundred dollars each! Our return flight was much better, with our luggage travelling with us this time.

CHAPTER 49

CHARLES AND NINA PARROTT

After the death of Peggy, Charles remarried Nina, and they settled in Honiton. Later, Nina's daughter Pam, persuaded them to move to a remote, tiny town of Llandbradach, just outside Caerphilly in Wales. It was here that Nina's health deteriorated; unable to walk without the aid of a walker, home help had to visit three times a day, while Charles did his best to accommodate her needs. After several mild heart attacks and visits to hospital, Nina was confined to a home where she could get the care that she needed. Meanwhile, Charles coped as best he could, and seemed to be managing well, when he collapsed at hospital after a check-up. He had suffered a massive heart attack and died at the age of ninety-two. Rosemary, Amanda, Sarah and Alex attended the funeral and had to deal with Pam and her husband Bill, who were not very helpful or friendly. It transpired that Bill had been charging Charles for taking him shopping, and even denied Charles a morning paper.

On previous visits, both Pam and Bill were putting pressure on Charles to give power of attorney (jointly) to Pam and Rosemary; Charles was reluctant to have this done, and was suspicious of the motives. On one subsequent visit to Wales, Charles was in hospital recovering from a minor complaint, but he was worried about his money. He told me that he had hidden £1500.00 in a bedroom draw, which was for me and Rosemary. On returning to the house, I found the money, but was interrupted by Bill who wanted to know what I was doing. I did not reveal what was going on, making some excuse about some clothes that Charles needed. The next door neighbour and her friend Mary were very kind to Charles in his final days, taking him shopping (no charge), preparing meals for both him and Nina, and always visiting and cheering them up. After his death, Rosemary was given £2000.00 cash, which Charles had given Mary to look after. It would seem that he was being robbed, and could not trust any of the relatives, not to mention whom! Nina lived on, surviving at a private home for the next few years, finally dying at the age of 101, when the estate was divided equally between the two daughters, Pam and Rosemary.

The death of Charles marked the end to a special time in my life. Over the years I had got to know him well, admiring his courage and honesty. He had been a POW in the Second World War, spending over four years in a camp, captured by the Italians, then handed over to the Germans. He had many stories to tell, yet only started to share them towards the end of his life. Initially, he was reported missing in action, and then presumed dead; however, six months later the Red Cross discovered where his group were. When he was captured he weighed two hundred pounds; surviving the four years in captivity, he was finally released and he weighed around one hundred pounds.

He shared one particular story with me about an event at the end of the war. The war was over, the Germans were surrendering, and the Americans could be seen from the prison camp, but it was not over yet. One of the prisoners made a run for the gate and was shot by a German guard. He was bleeding from the leg, and the commandant ordered Charles and another prisoner to get some medical aid from the Americans, as there were no supplies in the camp. They were told that they must return after taking the man on a stretcher. After arriving at the American lines, the other prisoner decided that he was not going back; Charles declared that he was, as he gave his word that he would return. Four hours later, two American soldiers dragged the guard in front of Charles, handing him a rifle and inviting him to beat him up. Charles refused, insisting that the guard had only done his duty, to stop a prisoner escaping. The two Americans snatched the rifle and beat the guard with it. Fortunately, a senior officer intervened and stopped this. Charles had to spend the first few months on a special farm in the West Country, learning how to eat again.

Charles and his brother Gilbert ran a fruit business, which was originally started by his father. The business was in Western

Super Mare. It began to thrive, with a fleet of vans, dealing with frozen food. Eventually, Findus food bought Charles and his brother out, and so they both retired. Gilbert bought a heavy equipment rental business, and Charles bought the Monkton Court Hotel, in Honiton Devon.

AFTERWORD

FINAL MOVE TO CALGARY

Having moved to Calgary, we enjoyed the frequent Chinook climate, and the scenery of the mountains close by. Living near to Alex and Kim, we were able to spend time with our two granddaughters, Kaitlin and Sophie. We have lost count of the number of moves we have made in our lives, but we most certainly don't lack variety. After fifty years of playing in both Anglican and Roman Catholic Churches, I am no longer playing the organ in church. Instead, I have focused my attention on teaching the violin and percussion to my two granddaughters.

Writing about my life, especially OHMS has been an enjoyable experience, meeting so many interesting characters over the past seventy years. I still miss my native England, having great difficulty in "laying my ghost", but now, Canada is my home after forty years. I return to the old country for brief visits; last year I went to a disappointing regimental reunion in Gloster, which convinced me that I made the right move in 1975, immigrating to Canada. However, I do miss, the sea, walking in the rain, bacon butties, wild daffodils, local bitter, pubs, and the British sense of humour. Here in Calgary, Canada, I am enjoying a better standard of living, fewer people, more space, the Chinook climate, mountains, driving and a more relaxed way of life. I heard someone say that "Calgary is the Hawaii of Canada".

Attempting to remember all the events of a lifetime was a difficult task, beginning first with separating my life into sections and moves; I found that looking at old photos would bring to mind an event, jogging the memory back to that particular time in life. Hopefully I have taken great care not to offend anyone, or dwell on the unhappy parts of my journey, always moving on to the next chapter in my life. As I approach my twilight years I have no regrets, and I know that there is more adventure ahead of me. For instance, volunteering my talents as a musician at Heritage Park in Calgary; playing the Harmonium in St Martin's church once a month and accompanying a soprano singer for some selected summer shows. I am tempted to stage yet another production of Handel's Messiah, but I have to choose the right moment to launch everything. I would like to thank my wife, Rosemary, for her encouragement with my book, and correcting some of my recollection of events. Looking over my work, there are some flips in time, which will hopefully make sense to the reader.

I am sure my grandchildren will have a good laugh reading some of the stories, and hopefully pass them on to their children. Having reached the young age of seventy-five, I now feel qualified to offer some pearls of wisdom regarding life. Make sure you follow your passion, laugh a lot, have faith, marry well, enjoy your children and remember they are the future, and we are the past. Family is important, and the most difficult task in life is to be able to say, "I love you". I found this awkward to say, which was probably due to my upbringing, but I always wanted to say it! Now is my chance: Rosemary, Clive, Amanda, Simon, Malcolm, Sarah, Emma, Julia and Alex, Kim, Nick, Marc, Celine, Terry, and Lucie. Grandchildren: Kaitlin, Sophie, Olivier, Adam, Evan, Shelby, Gabrielle, Christopher, Spencer, Nigel, Erin, Mark, Kirsten, Axcl, Reuben, Nicholas, Maia, Melissa, Aiden, and one great grandchild, Owen. *I LOVE YOU!*

"I leave you with one thought: Sometimes B sharp, Never B flat, but Always B natural. Viva la Music!"

Printed in Canada